AW
, de

By the Same Author

HOW TO BECOME A BISHOP
WITHOUT BEING RELIGIOUS

When
the
Saints
Go
Marching
Out

When the Saints Go Marching Out

Charles Merrill Smith

Illustrated by Robert Osborn

Doubleday & Company, Inc., Garden City, New York

1969

Library of Congress Catalog Card Number 69–15883
Copyright © 1969 by Charles Merrill Smith
All Rights Reserved
Printed in the United States of America

This is for my mother, Gladys Miller Smith,
and my father, the late Reverend Dr. Phillips Brooks Smith,
not saints, but something much better—loving parents.

Contents

BOOK TWO: THE STALWART CHRISTIANS

When the saints come marching in!
There is a terrific din!
Those contemplating this
splendid procession of martyrs,

                              virgins,

                                        and other

stalwart Christians,
praise their ways in verse
and worse.

On the other hand,
when the saints go marching out,
leaving the odor of sanctity
with the debris
of piety,
there is no doubt
—regrettably—
sin is in
but,
saints are something
we could just about
do without.

                              —Anonymous

How a Modern, Nonpious Man
Can Profit by Studying the Lives
of the Saints and Other Stalwart Christians

On the face of it nothing could be of less use to the man of
the computer age than a study of the lives of the saints. The
saints instruct the pious in ways and means of putting the heat
on heaven to let a chap in, methods of extracting approval
from the Almighty (apparently not easily come by), and other
payoffs for proper religious conduct. But will a careful perusal
of St. Vindicianus of Bullecourt show a fellow how to turn a
fast buck? Can a chapter a night from the biography of St.
Theophanes the Chronographer help us cope with crabgrass?
Of course not, you say. But you would be wrong.

It is our intent to demonstrate how you can get that promo-
tion, grab off the cash, win the game by the employment of
lessons learned from the lives of the saints. You no doubt think
this an unlikely claim, but keep reading.

We must begin by clarifying for you just what is a saint, and
the traditional or conventional use of his life and works.

A saint, technically, is a person of any sex who, through
exemplifying in his life the virtues and qualities prized by the
Roman Catholic branch of the Christian Church, has been
officially designated a saint by that sect. Other branches of
Christendom have their heroes too, although they have no
machinery for processing them into saints. But for practical
purposes they cannot be neglected, so we include a sample of

these nonofficial saints which we shall call "stalwart Christians."

The idea is that a saint has a parlay going for him—not only is he a cinch for heaven, but is also worthy of veneration and imitation here on earth. A saint, then, is a perpetual illustration of ideal religious conduct. Every saint has his feast day, which is the day he shuffled off this mortal coil, if known, or if not known somebody makes a guess as to the date of his departure and that becomes his feast day. When his feast day rolls around his virtues are recounted, and the congregation is urged to emulate him.

Since it will be helpful if we have a thorough grasp of the saint business let us look at an example of how the system works. It is best that, for purposes of illustration, we make up a saint. Though imaginary, our biography will be in the literary style favored by chroniclers of the lives of the saints.

St. Chastitus The Austere (d. 1121)

December 10

Born of a poor family in Pibrac, near Toulouse, Chastitus was known as Jacques the Tanner because he earned his living as a tanner's assistant. He was indolent at his work, spending all his time with barmaids, kitchen slaveys, and other women of the lower classes and loose morals. It is said that by the time he was twenty-four years of age he had fathered more than a hundred illegitimate children, although some authorities claim the number did not exceed fifty.

In his forty-eighth year, while suffering from a severe case of the pox, he had a vision of the devil coming to drive him to hell in a red-hot chariot. He was so frightened by this vision that he immediately took Holy Orders, chose the name Chastitus as a sign that he had forsaken his former ways, and vowed never to look at a woman again.

Assigned as a gardener's helper at a small monastery in Brittany, his humble suggestions for improving the administration of the monastery earned him the enmity of his superiors, so he decided to found his own order. Through his energy, administrative skill, and long hours put in at his work, the Abnegation Fathers, as he named the order, was soon the leading order in Central Europe. It was St. Chastitus who first had the idea of expanding a single monastery into a chain, with centralized administration, purchasing, and accounting. Abnegation Fathers follow the rule of averting the eyes when in the presence of women, and of allowing themselves only one slice of bread, of a uniform size, per meal.

St. Chastitus died at the age of ninety-one, leaving a reputation for extreme austerity of life and the richest monastic order in Christendom.

The normal Christian employment of the life of St. Chastitus would be to scare the hell out of anyone indulging in unsanctioned hanky-panky. On St. Chastitus' feast day the preacher, or the teacher in the parochial school, by judicious use of the life of St. Chastitus, could easily frighten the younger children just beginning to feel their oats. The older boys and girls would think twice before disappearing into the hedgerows for a frolic lest they contract the pox or an unwanted pregnancy. And wayward husbands and wives of the pious sort would be lashed with guilt feelings and, maybe, visions of the devil coming to get them, and either cut out their cavorting or at least spend much time (and money) in church in quest of absolution.

Parish pastors were too realistic to expect that by reciting the life of St. Chastitus they could eliminate sex completely. But by injecting a lot of fear and anxiety into it they hoped to keep it within manageable bounds, plus promoting business at the confessional, since there is nothing better than a lively sense of sin to keep a church thriving.

Since Christendom has, up to now, a collection of some twenty thousand certified saints, the various books devoted to their dossiers offer a vast smorgasbord of virtues, attributes, pieties, etc., from which the instructor may choose to make his point.

If, say, he wants to drive home the blessedness of poverty, not the easiest of virtues to promote, he has only to trot out St. Francis of Assisi, who was much happier broke than loaded. Or if he contemplates a hot sermon on the sinfulness of high-fashion clothes, St. Ethelreda comes immediately to mind[1] as prime homiletical material. Or a stout defense of doctrinal accuracy, one of the most cherished of Christian virtues, would inevitably recall St. Anatolius of Constantinople.[2] Such renowned religious attributes as piety, long-suffering, continence, poverty, learning, ignorance, virginity, orthodoxy, fasting, contributing to the needs of the Church, misery, chastity, and a veritable avalanche more, can easily be taught

[1] Not to be confused with St. Etheldreda, sometimes known as St. Alfrida. St. Ethelreda, sometimes known as St. Audrey, was, you will no doubt recall, the daughter of Anna, King of East Anglia, and the sister of Sts. Willeburga, Sexburga, and Ethelburga. Though highly thought of in saintly circles, she "wore inconvenient and clumsy clothing."

[2] He was the one who, when the Nestorians and the Eutyches were killing each other over their theological differences, bravely tried to make these Christian warriors accept Pope Leo's true definition of Christological doctrine. You would not want to get him mixed up with St. Anatolius of Laodicea, of course, who spent his time fooling around with arithmetic, geometry, astronomy, and Aristotelian philosophy.

through the lives of the saints, what with a clutch (or more) of saints handy to illustrate each virtue.

Alas! The saints, for all their redoubtable record as instructors to countless millions in how to live the religious life in an unreligious world, have fallen to a state of neglect. Protestants have always been unaccountably reluctant to utilize these heroes of the faith—except, of course, for the apostles and, occasionally, Joseph and Mary. But even the Romans now tend to pay only lip service to the saints, and it is reliably reported that hagiography gets less and less attention in Catholic seminaries with each passing year.[3]

Though staunchly Protestant, the author has been long an admirer of and student of the saints, and has for several years been depressed over their neglect. Obviously a reason for this shameful shelving of the saints is wanting, and one now has emerged.

Not long ago, watching an exciting episode of *Peyton Place* on television and simultaneously skimming *The Wall Street Journal* while idly sipping a sarsaparilla, the author was struck by the insight that we now live in a secular age, and the old pieties so well exemplified by the lives of the saints are out of style. Secular man lives by secular values, quite different than the virtues of the saints which moved an earlier time to emulation.

[3] "These young squirts of priests just don't know their hagiography any more," an R.C. bishop of the author's acquaintance said recently. "Why, in my day," he continued, "any of us could have snapped out a paragraph—from memory, mind you—on Sts. Leodager, Cyril, Secundus, Eleutherious, or almost any saint you can name. Nowadays you're hard put to find a priest under thirty-five who can distinguish between St. Fortunatus of Todi and St. Dominic Loricatus."

Yet does not secular man need heroes too? Is he not just as anxious for a divine certification of the values he lives by? Doesn't he long for saints to imitate? Of course he does.

At this point in his ruminations the author was the recipient of a revelation. Was it possible that the lives of the saints contained, in addition to the standard religious lessons, unmined veins of secular wisdom? A hasty examination of a handy hagiography showed that indeed they did. The secular[4] lessons are there in abundance, heretofore undiscovered because no one had the wit to look for them.

Let us examine, in detail, how we extract lessons for living, guides to achievement in today's world, principles, which if followed with the same faithfulness and devotion accorded the pieties of St. Sulpicius the Wise, or Blessed Elizabeth Picenardi by an earlier age, will yield the modern imitator of religious heroes the twentieth-century equivalent of spiritual security, peace of mind, and a condition of general blessedness which rewarded the faithful in the days when St. Methodius of Thessalonica was going strong.

The reader will recall that we have pointed out, in the case of our made-up saint, St. Chastitus the Austere, that old-style use of his life for Christian pedagogy would be to illustrate the unfulfilling results, downright painful consequences, and general undesirability of making too big a thing of sex. In the sporting period of Chastitus' life, sex is linked with indolence, the fathering of innumerable bastards, and the pox. The clincher, though, is the devil coming for him in a red-hot chariot. The lesson is as obvious as Zsa Zsa Gabor's accent: Sex will damn you to hell.

[4] In the interest of precision we use the term "secular" as the dictionary defines it: "Of or pertaining to worldly things, or things not regarded as spiritual or religious."

Life would be considerably less complicated for the modern preacher if he could rely on such lessons from the lives of the saints to do the job they once did. But they will not. Our modern secularized man, good Christian though he may be, knows that most ladies of an acquiescent disposition are on the pill, so the issue of illegitimate offsprings is unlikely to occur from a liaison of the moment. He also has great faith in the potency of antibiotics to cure any type of the pox he might carelessly pick up. And with sentimental contemporary theologians assuring him that the Almighty doesn't believe in hell, he has no fears of going there.

So it would seem that St. Chastitus has had his day as an instructor, that he is finished. And so he has, if we utilize his life according to traditional methods of explication.

But, substituting the secular principle for the religious, we find, happily, that the facts are capable of reinterpretation.

We have, for example, the fact that when Chastitus was indulging himself with the congenial maidens of the vicinity he was indolent and entirely unsuccessful economically. The old-style preacher would interpret this as God's judgment on Chastitus' sinful habits.

As we have seen, such an interpretation would elicit a hearty horse laugh from a modern, sophisticated secular man. But let us ask ourselves the question, "Why was Chastitus indolent and unsuccessful in his business when chasing women, but energetic and spectacularly successful when he cut out his fooling around?"

The answer is obvious: When every day included passionate hours spent with some floozie (or floozies), Chastitus was always tired. Anyone would be. No less an authority than Napoleon Hill has pointed out that many a potential corporate executive or captain of industry has dissipated a promising

career in the bedroom.[5] Put in this way, our secularized man
will listen with rapt attention to the argument. Punishment for
sins bores him, but this gets him where he lives. We have discarded a theological or pietistic reason for Chastitus' indolence
and adopted a physiological explanation. This the secular man
can grasp. He may well have been wondering why he's been
dragging around lately. Couple this with a glowing description
of Chastitus' enormous success in his postconcupiscent period
and you have presented, for the average ambitious, upwardly
mobile, normally greedy middle-class secular man a seductive
and well-nigh irresistible argument for behaving himself. Of
course, we must face it that if this kind of religious instruction
became widespread it would no doubt issue in wholesale dis-
carding of mistresses, underemployment of ladies of the evening, and even a sharp increase in the number of neglected
wives. But then, all progress exacts its price.

Let us, then, compare the lessons to be derived by a study
of the life of St. Chastitus as a pious reader of an earlier time
would see them, with the wisdom a modern, secular man
would distill from it.

The old-style lessons, condensed, would read something like
this:

(a) God will surely punish sinners, especially those who
    indulge in unsanctified sex.

(b) God will reward pious living and spiritual endeavors
    with great rewards, here as well as hereafter.

On the other hand, the new-style secular reader would infer from these same facts set forth in the life of St. Chastitus
these lessons:

[5] Mr. Hill, no moralist, sees time spent in the conjugal bed or
ménage of the mistress as equally reprehensible so far as business
success is concerned.

(a) Sex is fun, but it requires a sinful amount of time and energy.

(b) If you want to pile up the bucks, or be president of the corporation, you have to put first things first.

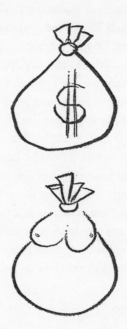

The perceptive reader will immediately grasp that the two sets of lessons bring us out at substantially the same place. But whereas the old-style lessons were designed to appeal to the aspirations of the pious (avoidance of punishment for sins, especially escaping hell, and gaining the approval of the Almighty), the new-style lessons sock it to the secularized man at the center of his concern (mainly, achieving success, and especially the symbols of success). In either case we get, as our end product, conformity to predetermined standards of personal behavior which, of course, is what makes for an easily controllable and culturally desirable society. And who can argue that this has always been true religion's ultimate goal and finest contribution to human life?

The author would encourage the reader to get himself any one of the standard *Lives of the Saints* and develop the ability to read them with an eye for selecting not the pious but the secular lessons from them.[6] To stimulate the practice we will now proceed to offer a representative sample of saints, with the secular lessons listed at the end of each "life" in concise, pithy form just as old-style hagiographies list the pious lessons. Anyone who reads these carefully will soon get the hang of it.

The reader must realize that many saints' names, attached to noble and esteemed figures in the history of the faith though they are, fall strangely on the modern ear. Such noneuphonius cognomens as Sts. Winwallus, Kunigunde, Madoald, Turibius, Deogratius, Blessed Notker Balbulus the Stammerer,[7] not to mention Sts. Fraimbault, Sebaldus, Lizier, and Blessed Gobert might tempt the reader to suspect that the saints hereinafter described are put-ons, manufactured by the author out of his vivid and creative imagination. They are not. Each and every one is a real saint and can be found in any reasonably complete hagiography or martyrology.

Furthermore, the facts and evidence which make up their biographies are faithfully reproduced here by the author in a

[6] If pressed for time, he can legitimately do this in the hours formerly used for devotional reading. In fact, the author is contemplating starting "a saint a day" program as an aid to the unimaginative and the lazy. Watch for further details.

[7] Since he couldn't talk very good, he wrote a *Life of Charlemagne*, a *Martyrology*, and numerous sequences—whatever they are.

manner reflecting his impeccable scholarship. A certain selectivity has been exercised, so far as the facts are concerned, in the interests of brevity and readability. An occasionally modern idiom has been employed in reporting, for example, a conversation between a saint and the devil where available records appear to be inexact. These liberties are a scholar's prerogative.

The author owes something to the scholarly style of that great naturalist and historian, the late Will Cuppy, author of such outstanding works as *How To Tell Your Friends from the Apes* and *The Decline and Fall of Practically Everybody*, especially his distinctive use of the footnote.[8] Also a smattering, or at least a soupçon of James Thurber might be detected in our manner of drawing the lessons from the lives of the saints.

We are certain, however, that the brilliance, originality, and distinctive style of these "lives" is so apparent as to make this alone a sufficient reason for purchasing this book. The incalculable blessings awaiting the reader who digests and applies to his life the lessons herein contained is, then, a bonus, and for the author (though he anticipates a phenomenal sale of the hardback edition, plus a profitable market for first and second serial rights, and of course, paperback reprints) more than ample reward for the arduous hours spent in scholarly research and unmeasurable toil invested in writing and rewriting[9] this significant book.

[8] This is a valid form of thievery, for has not T. S. Eliot assured us that "Bad poets borrow, but good poets steal outright."?

[9] With the help of Barbara Allen, a typist whose patience should qualify her for sainthood.

Book One

The Blessed Saints

St. George

No doubt St. Francis, the evangelists, and some of the apostles are more familiar to us today than St. George, but over the long haul he has generated more pious enthusiasm than perhaps any other saint.

Other than that he was martyred at Lydda in Palestine cir. 303, we know nothing whatever about him except that he once killed a dragon near Silena in Libya. The true facts, as accurately rendered as research makes possible, seem to be these:

This dragon lived in a lake, but came out every so often snorting fire and knocking down things, and in general making a nuisance of itself. The town finally struck a bargain with the dragon. The town would provide two sheep per day for the dragon.[1] In return, the dragon would leave the town alone.

---

[1] One for lunch, and one for dinner. We don't know what the dragon did for breakfast or between-meal snacks.

The town also tried to kill the dragon by sending out armies to fight it, but the dragon always won. Sometimes, when sheep were scarce, the town would substitute one of the village maidens. These girls were chosen by drawing straws or some other form of lottery, and it was not considered a great honor to be the dragon's menu for the day.

One day, the King's daughter drew the unlucky number and was about to be served up to the dragon when George, who wasn't a saint yet, came riding through town. He sized up the situation, made the sign of the cross, and went galloping off after the dragon. When he found it, the dragon came at George with its mouth wide open, sending up lots of smoke and fire and looking something awful. This made it difficult for the dragon to see, so George whacked it with his lance, and it promptly toppled over dead.

George then rode back to town and preached a sermon, and all the citizens were converted and baptized. The King offered George a huge reward, but he told the King to give it to the poor.

St. George is popular everywhere, but somehow he appeals to the English the most. In 1222 the National Council at Oxford established a holy day of obligation in his honor, which —by order of the Archbishop of Canterbury—was later given the same religious weight as Christmas.[2] King Edward III founded the still-prestigious Order of the Knights of St. George, which is known today as Knights of the Garter for reasons so complicated that only an Englishman can understand them.

---

[2] The English like Christmas better, though.

The Lessons

St. George was a practical-type saint from whose life we learn:

(a) Dragons look pretty scary, but they seldom live up to advance notices.

(b) Capable dragon-slayers are always in great demand, but they cost more today.

(c) There is no way to beat Christmas as a pious holiday unless you come up with something that has better commercial possibilities.

(d) Dragons, and people, would get in less trouble if they learned to keep their mouths shut.

Blessed[1] Cunegundes

All we know of Blessed Cunegundes is that she was a Franciscan tertiary, and that she was canonized because, though she was the wife of King Boleslaus V (of Poland), she lived with him in "perpetual continence."[2]

[1] "Blessed" is a pious brevet bestowed on Stalwart Christians not quite of the first chop.

[2] Biographies of saints exhibit a commendable delicacy in their literary style.

The Lesson

One would think that Boleslaus was a more logical candidate for sainthood than Cunegundes, but the world has a way of misplacing its rewards.

Blessed Pellegrino

Of noble birth, Pellegrino was converted by St. Francis of Assisi and spent his life as a lay brother in the order of Franciscans, where he specialized in piety and humility. He is still invoked to cure toothache.

The Lesson

You can win a certain amount of local renown for piety and humility, but for an international reputation and an undying place in history, a toothache cure is better.

St. Philomena

Christendom has seldom, if ever, seen so spectacular a rise to fame, popularity, and well-nigh universal veneration as that of St. Philomena. Fortunately we know a great deal about her, as there are libraries practically full of books on St. Philomena, although you could find out all you need to know on the subject in a snappy little volume by Don Francesco di Lucia, the priest who transported the sacred remains of the virgin martyr from Rome to Mugnano in 1805.[1]

To give you the facts in barest outline form, Philomena lived in Rome during the third century, and was—at the age of twelve or thirteen—still a virgin[2] as well as a Christian.

The Emperor, it seems, got awfully irritated with Philomena because, her biographers say, he lusted after her[3] and Philomena said no dice. To get her in a more receptive mood the Emperor had her dragged through the streets of Rome, but this didn't change Philomena's attitude, so they threw her in the pokey overnight and the next day dragged her around some more. When Philomena told the Emperor it was still no dice he had his bowmen heat their arrows to red hot and told them to shoot at her, but the arrows just made a loop like

[1] Its title is *Relazione Istorica della Traslazione del Sacro Corpo e Miracoli di Santo Filomena, Vergine Martire, da Rome a Mugnano del Cardinale.*

[2] You may think it not unusual for a girl to be a virgin at twelve or thirteen, but you don't know your third-century Romans.

[3] Roman Emperors at that time did a great deal of lusting.

a bomerang and killed six of the guys who were shooting them, and the other bowmen declined to shoot at her any more, for which you can't blame them too much. So the Emperor put her in a dungeon and tied her to a pole and made one last pass at her with no better luck than he had had before, so he had her killed with a spear.

This fascinating story was completely unknown until May of 1802 when, it is said, through the intervention of Our Lady, Help of Christians, some workmen uncovered her tomb. All the more miraculous is the ingenious way scholars deduced the story from nothing more than the inscription on the tomb and an artifact or two in it.

The inscription on the tomb read LUMENA PAXTE FI, which doesn't make sense in Latin or any other language, but scholars said that it was obvious to anyone with a grain of sense that the stonemason had gotten the slabs mixed up and that if you just switched them around the inscription would read PAX TECUM FILUMENA, and that translates out to "Peace be to you, Philomena," which seems reasonable enough. The slabs also had on them an anchor, some arrows, and a palm. These symbols mean that it is a Christian buried here because an anchor is shaped sort of like a cross, and also that the Emperor had tied an anchor around Philomena's neck and thrown her in the Tiber, but the angels cut the cords binding the anchor to her and she floated, although the anchor didn't.[4] The arrows mean that she was shot at with arrows, which certainly doesn't strain our credulity. The palm is supposed to represent a mystic lily, whatever a mystic lily is, and also a virgin's lamp, or maybe both, but I'm not sure why.

[4] Biographers of Philomena assure us that the anchor is still resting on the bottom of the Tiber, but no one has found it yet.

We must remember, though, that it isn't so much the details of a saint's life which makes for the saint's popularity. It is the miracles which a saint can perform for you. And when it comes to miracles Philomena is gangbusters. Some saints specialize, and are invoked only for toothache or athlete's foot, or disorders of the large intestine. Philomena, it seems, can do damn near anything and, as one of her faithful followers has put it, nothing is too important and nothing is too trivial for her. We have it on incontrovertible authority that she has cured an inguinal rupture, sore eyes, kidney stones, a broken leg, and countless other afflictions of the flesh. She is also pretty strong against barrenness and has helped thousands of women get pregnant.

Nor does she confine herself to the physical maladies of life. She is much opposed to divorce, and if invoked by a couple about to split up, will usually patch up the sagging marriage, thus relieving the couple of the unpleasant necessity for marriage counseling, lawyer's fees, etc. She has been known to prevent a robbery. And one time she appeared to a dying priest holding out a bishop's miter to him, and he immediately sprang from his bed, and in no time became a bishop.[5] Philomena is especially popular with pious Italian ladies, and they call on her to do something about a son who has been negligent in attendance at mass, to persuade a daughter to take the veil, to cut a husband's excessive thirst for Chianti, or to handle any of the other aches and pains of life, whether physical or spiritual, and Philomena usually comes through, so no wonder she is a contender for, or winner of, the title of

[5] Cynics have claimed that the prospects of a bishopric will shoot massive amounts of adrenalin into the nervous system of any obscure priest and return him to health practically when *rigor mortis* has set in. But you know how cynics are.

Most Reliable of Christian Saints and is, without doubt, the most versatile.

Unfortunately, very recent research has revealed that the scholars who uncovered the story of Philomena had one or two of their facts wrong, and the Vatican now says that St. Philomena probably never existed at all.

The Lessons

The heart-warming, charming story of St. Philomena teaches us an almost endless number of helpful lessons, a few of which are:

(a) Scholarly research is one of the true boons to mankind, but some researchers are more reliable than others.

(b) If you want the world's acclaim in sainthood or anything else, you have to deliver the goods.

(c) When defending your virginity, red-hot arrows may not harm you, but it is best not to count on it.

(d) In matters of faith, it apparently works just as well if you believe in something that doesn't exist as if you believe in something that does.

St. Polycarp

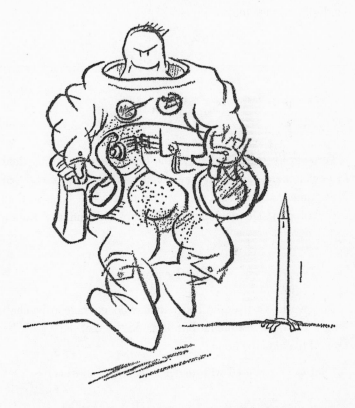

St. Polycarp lived eighty-six years, and when he was condemned to be burned alive he didn't mind because he had divine assurance that the flames would not harm him. Sure enough, they didn't, but the officials put out the fire and had him stabbed to death.

The Lesson

Everyone ought to have fire insurance, but you need other kinds of coverage too.

St. Perfecto[1]

Perfecto lived in Cordova at the time when the Arabs were in power there. One day they asked him what he thought of Mohammed, and he said that Mohammed was a fake, so they executed him. He died cursing Mohammed and the Koran.

The Lesson

The world vastly admires a man who courageously challenges the establishment, but it is likely that he won't be around to enjoy the honor.

[1] Not to be confused with the cigar of the same name.

St. Macarius the Younger

In the third century an awful lot of hermits and holy men hung around the Egyptian desert, and most of them were named Macarius.[1] Because of this, St. Macarius was referred to as "the Younger," to distinguish him from the other Macarii. He embarked early in life on a career as a sugar-plum merchant, which is what they called a baker in the third century, but at the age of forty he forsook his shop and ovens, possibly because of the heat, or maybe it was acid indigestion, and withdrew into the desert at Nitria. (After getting himself ordained as a priest. Ordination is a genuine status symbol among holy hermits, most of whom never went to seminary.) He was soon recognized as a real comer in the hermit business, and was forever being pointed out to tourists as one who had risen rapidly in piety and spiritual knowledge—so rapidly, in fact, that he incurred the hostility of the devil and his bishop (a patriarch named Lucius), suffering much from each.[2]

Macarius seems to have been a Renaissance man considerably before the Renaissance. In addition to having mastered the sugar-plum profession, he is reputed to have been a fountain of spiritual knowledge, adept at surviving in the desert, a poet, and a charmer of animals. His friend Pallas relates the following incident: One day a mother hyena brought to

[1] In the third century you could go out in the Egyptian desert and yell, "Hey, Mac" and collect quite a congregation.

[2] His biographers do not tell us from which of these he suffered most.

Macarius her newborn cub which was blind. Macarius petted it, and the cub opened its eyes.[3] The next day the mother hyena came back with a magnificent sheepskin in her mouth and presented it to Macarius as an expression of her gratitude. Macarius was so touched by this gesture[4] that he made it into a tunic which he wore for the rest of his life, although considering that he lived to be a hundred, the tunic must have gotten pretty smelly.

The *Lausiac History*, a work of unassailable authority, reveals that Macarius one day crossed the Nile by boat and was so joyful of countenance that the boatman inquired why he was so happy though obviously dead broke. Macarius replied, "It is because I despise this world, of which you are the slave, as much as it deserves." The boatman decided Macarius was on to a good thing and went into the hermit business himself.

The Lessons

We learn from the inspiring life of St. Macarius the Younger:
(a) The life of a sugar-plum merchant can't be much if the Egyptian desert is better.
(b) It is admirable to be a poet and to have a way with animals, but there is very little market for it.
(c) The world may well be as despicable as Macarius thought it to be, but if too many boatmen become convinced of this, getting across rivers is going to be a problem.

[3] Skeptics have claimed that hyenas are born blind and that the cub would have opened its eyes in due time anyway, but this ruins the story.

[4] Hyenas are in some ways superior to people.

St. Eulalia of Mérida[1]

St. Eulalia, who was martyred at about the age of thirteen, didn't like games, toys, fine clothes, jewelry, or the smell of roses. What she did like was the idea of martyrdom. When the Emperor Diocletian issued an edict that all Christians had to burn pig's liver before pagan idols, she saw her chance. She went to call on Calpurnian, prefect of Mérida, and announced that she was not going to burn pig's liver to idols.[2] So Calpurnian burned her instead. She is remembered today because the poet Prudentius wrote a hymn in her honor. "Never has a human creature been endowed with more grace or fascination," is what he wrote.

The Lessons

(a) When a thirteen-year-old kid shows an interest in being burned alive, you'd better hustle her off to the psychiatrist.

[1] Not to be confused with St. Eulalia of Barcelona. Since the two saints lived at exactly the same time and their biographies are identical, even to martyrdom at the same age, it is not always easy to keep them separate in our minds. Scholars assure us, however, that there were two Eulalias—which, in view of their lives, would seem to be all the Eulalias we need.

[2] She spit in his face, too.

(b) For permanent publicity, a bad poem is better than a good news story.

St. Isidore of Seville

St. Isidore is called St. Isidore of Seville because he was born at Seville or Cartagena, we don't know which. He was the younger brother of Sts. Leander, Fulgentius, and Florentina, but he was awfully dumb and was always flunking out of school. In fact, he played hooky a lot, because every day at school included at least one beating by an exasperated teacher.

Isidore despaired of getting anywhere in the world by the use of his mind, so he entered the Church and became a bishop. He was the bishop of Seville for forty years. He converted the Arian Goths, kept the Acephalous Heretics from propagating their errors,[1] and founded a magnificent college and put himself on the faculty as Professor of Holy Scriptures and Profane Authors. He wrote many erudite books, among them the *Historia de Regibus* and the *Mozarabic Liturgy*.

[1] They were shaky on Christological doctrine.

The Lesson

The one shining gem of a lesson to be mined from the life of St. Isidore is this: If you want to get ahead in the world but you aren't very bright, it is best to own the business.

Sts. Theodora and Didymus

These two saints are listed together, for it is doubtful if either would have achieved blessedness without the other.

Theodora was a noble lady of Alexandria in the days of the Emperor Diocletian. One day Proculus, the prefect of Alexandria, called her in and said, "Theodora, why aren't you married, seeing as how you are free, white, twenty-one, and a real knockout?"

Theodora replied that since she was strongly prejudiced in favor of virginity, she intended to remain an old maid.

The prefect said that the Emperor did not share her views on virginity and had ordered that all nubile Christian maidens[1] who persisted in the spinster state were to be consigned to one of the local brothels.[2]

Theodora, evidently a stubborn type, said, "Nuts, Proculus." The prefect, a patient man, argued with her. Don't disgrace

[1] The good-looking ones, anyway.
[2] Perhaps Diocletian owned a piece of the business.

your family, why be a nonconformist, things like that, is what he told her.

But Theodora wouldn't change her mind, so they packed her off to the red-light district.

As she was entering the establishment which was to be her new home, a Christian soldier named Didymus spoke to her, saying, "The first reason I am here is to save you." He didn't mention his second reason for being there. Didymus instructed her to change clothes with him and then blow the area, which she did.[3]

Didymus was turned over to the authorities by his first customer.[4] He was beheaded and his body burned. St. Ambrose tells us that Theodora voluntarily turned herself in and was also beheaded.

The Lessons

Very few saints' lives offer us the down-to-earth, nitty-gritty lessons to be found in the biographies, however brief, of Theodora and Didymus. Among them are:

(a) Virginity may well be worthy and commendable, but why overdo a good thing?

(b) You can fight city hall, but you're likely to lose.

(c) Never trust a disappointed sport.

[3] One would think that this sight would have stopped the crowds, but then, Alexandrians are reputed to be as unshockable as the residents of Greenwich Village.

[4] This is what his biographers say, honest. What this ancient, unnamed sport actually said when Theodora turned out to be Didymus the scholars do not tell us—which is probably just as well.

(d) If you hang around houses of ill-repute, you may lose
your head.

St. Philemon the Flutist

Early in the fourth century there was in Egypt a chap
named Philemon who was a very bad flute player. But as it
takes an expert to tell a good flute player from a bad flute

player, he was very popular and something of a public hero much as Rock Hudson and other bad actors are today. However, he gave up the flute and took up Christianity instead, and the prefect Hierocles had him thrown into the sea.

The Lesson

It may be better to be a good Christian than a bad flutist, but bad flutists are more appreciated by the public than good Christians.

Blessed Giles of Santarém

Son of a royal governor, Giles spent his early youth studying at the University of Coimbra and picking up for himself all the rich benefices[1] in the neighborhood which happened to fall vacant. Some historians say these were the just rewards of outstanding scholarship, while others say it may have a connection with the fact that he was the governor's son. Finally, he acquired a particularly wealthy abbey and, quitting school, moved in as head man. He found the duties of running an abbey, which involved spending a lot of time in church

[1] These were heavily endowed parishes, abbeys, and assorted ecclesiastical posts. An avid collector of benefices had himself the equivalent of a whopping block of Xerox or Data Processing.

chanting plain song, not much to his liking, so he took off for Paris to take up the study of medicine,[2] leaving, of course, a forwarding address where his checks were to be sent.

As he neared his destination he met the devil, who is reputed to have his headquarters in Paris, who said to him, "Giles, you're my type of guy. How's about I show you a lot of devilish secrets which will make it a snap for you to gain the honors and pleasures of the world?"

"What's in it for you?" Giles asked.

"Just sign this paper which says 'I renounce my baptism to become a servant of Satan,'" the devil replied.

"Fair enough," Giles said, and signed.

The devil kept his end of the bargain, for Giles soon became known as the most learned and—what's far more difficult in Paris—the most debauched man in town. All this study and helling around was hard on his constitution, though, and one night, suffering from general debility,[3] he had a dream in which he was in the cemetery back at his abbey and a bunch of spectres were hopping around on the tombs and yelling, "Woe to thee, if thou changest not thy life."[4] Waking up in a cold sweat, he repented of his debauchery.[5] So he went to confession, joined the Dominicans, and went to live in a monastery in Portugal. It is said that he became an eloquent preacher, and that he was especially efficacious in converting the most dedicated of sinners. As a reward for his exemplary, if belated, piety, the Virgin snatched his signed renunciation

[2] That's what he told them at the abbey, anyway.

[3] Or it may have been DT's.

[4] Spectres talk funny.

[5] A large hangover is a powerful argument for improving one's habits.

from the devil[6] and delivered it to him in the choirstall where he was chanting plain song.

The Lessons

The life of Blessed Giles is replete with practical lessons for daily living, from which abundance we cull the following:

    (a) For an excellent start in life, nothing is more helpful than having a rich father.

    (b) Both scholarship and debauchery are more beneficial when taken in moderate doses.

    (c) Sermons against sin apparently have more horsepower when the preacher knows what he is talking about.

    (d) You can beat the devil sometimes, but don't count on it.

Blessed Oliver Plunket

Oliver Plunket was Catholic primate of Ireland in the middle of the seventeenth century when the Protestants were going strong. They accused him of taxing his clergy to raise an army to fight England, so he was taken to London and hung. His last words were, "It is good for me at this time to give an example to the Irish people, since I have already given them so much good advice."

[6] Transported saints are not bound by the ethical considerations which hamper mortals.

The Lesson

There is no denying the power of personal example, but you seldom get hung just for giving good advice.

Blessed John Jones

John Jones was a Welshman who went to college in Rome and became a priest while there. When he came back to Wales, the people accused him of "being ordained abroad" and hung him.

The Lesson

A European education is a terrific status symbol, but the neighbors may think you are a snob.

St. Christina the Astonishing

It is difficult to ascertain the facts in the life of St. Christina the Astonishing because so many of her biographers record well-nigh incredible events and acts connected with her piety. We should be extremely critical, for example, of the biographical data reported by Thomas de Cantimpré, who tells us about all sorts of miracles and stuff Christina is supposed to have done, but which outrage our sense of the possible and probable. Though he was Professor of Theology at the University of Louvain, he was known to be a credulous type, which is an occupational failing since theologians are notorious suckers for fairy tales, especially when the fairy tales support their pet doctrines.

Cardinal Jacques de Vitry, on the other hand, is a more reliable chronicler. Administrators are hard-headed, practical men not as easily deluded as professors. In addition to his manifest competence as a researcher, the cardinal knew St. Christina personally and was therefore able to vouch for the facts.

He tells us that though Christina had been dead a long time, she had been granted the grace of "resuming the flesh," or what we of a more scientific age would call reincarnation, so that she could spend her years of purgatory on earth.

In her reincarnated form Christina passed the time in such worthwhile activities as rolling in the fire, remaining in icy waters in the middle of winter, walking among the tombs of the dead, and, in moments of extraordinary ecstasy, leading the souls of the dead into purgatory.[1] On days when her ecstasy was at its highest horsepower she would lead souls from purgatory to paradise, which is said to be an unusually hazardous trip.

It should not go unnoted that the smell of sin nauseated

[1] Cardinal de Vitry does not tell us if these souls appreciated Christina's efforts.

her, and after sniffing it, it was a long time before she could stand her fellow men.

The Lessons

(a) Sober, reliable chroniclers such as Cardinal de Vitry deserve the world's appreciation, for without them history would be nothing but a pack of wild tales.

(b) Reincarnation, or a second shot at life, isn't what it's cracked up to be.

(c) Being nauseated by the smell of sin is indeed a virtue, but it does limit your choice of vocation.

Blessed Villano

Villano was a Camaldulite monk of Font-Avellana who later became bishop of Gubbio, his hometown. All we know of this famous churchman is that it was in his diocese during his incumbency that St. Francis converted a wolf.

The Lesson

You don't really have to do anything to get yourself remembered by history if you can manage to be in the neighborhood when history is happening.

St. Nicholas of Flue

St. Nicholas had a wife and ten children, and one day he went out to a hermitage and stayed for nineteen years.

The Lesson

If you have a houseful of noisy kids, a wife should expect that her husband sometimes may need to get away for a little vacation.

St. Rayner the Troubadour

St. Rayner, who was born at Pisa early in the twelfth century, is known as "the troubadour" because he was a troubadour. He would take to the road and along about dinnertime would stop at a likely looking castle and offer to furnish dinner music in exchange for bed, board, and tips.[1] Rayner would accompany himself on the viol.[2]

[1] Since this helped the gentry pass the long, boring evenings, they considered it a bargain.

[2] Similar to a violin, but with deeper ribs, at least six strings, sloping shoulders, and frets. These are important differences, but no one knows why.

One evening, in the castle of a noble lady where he was singing his ballads, Rayner met Albert of Corsica[3], who offered to pray for Rayner. Rayner gladly accepted, since even in those days show business people were suckers for a little religion now and then. Albert evidently knew his business, for Rayner, a naturally cheerful type, was overcome with a sense of his sinfulness, threw his viol in the fire, shut himself up in a room of the castle, and wept day and night for his sins. In fact, he wept so much that he suffered from temporary blindness, and it is said that the radical change in his conduct led people to think that he had gone mad. William James would have delighted in Rayner's symptoms, and no doubt would have included him in *The Varieties of Religious Experience;* unfortunately, James wasn't around at the time.

But it all turned out for the best. Rayner, perceiving the error of his frivolous, joyous ways, renounced troubadouring, settled down, and became a sober merchant, at which—according to his biographer, Beninseca—he quickly made a lot of money.[4]

One day, though, he opened his well-filled purse and, according to eminently reliable historians, "such a stink came out that Rayner immediately scented the devil" and decided that from then on he would do entirely without money.

He returned to Pisa where he freeloaded for a while off the canons regular, then entered the monastery of St. Guy where he died highly thought of but without estate.

[3] We know that Albert was a holy man, but we don't know what he was doing at a twelfth-century hoedown instead of being in a monastery or out in the desert. There is a mystery here.

[4] If American middle-class Protestants ever need a patron saint they should consider St. Rayner.

The Lessons

It is evident from the thrilling biography of St. Rayner the Troubadour that

(a) Troubadouring, as a profession, isn't much, but it can lead to some profitable connections.

(b) Weeping for one's sins has a pious value, but it can cause eye trouble.

(c) A sound religious conversion and making pots of money often go hand-in-hand.

(d) It is hard for rich people to avoid guilt feelings over their prosperity.

(e) The devil has a distinctive smell, but he may have started using deodorants.

St. Austregisilus

All we know of the life of St. Austregisilus is that one time his friends were insisting that he ought to be married and he replied, "If I found a good wife I would be too afraid of losing her; and if you want me to have a bad one, I would rather not."

The Lesson

From this fragmentary record of the life of St. Austregisilus, we can never forget that while there are very few good arguments in favor of the celibate life, there are some.

St. Maximus of Turin

St. Maximus was a contemporary of St. Augustine, and it was thought at the time that future generations would consider his life and his literary works the superior of St. Augustine's, but they didn't.

The Lesson

Picking a winner was just as tough in the fifth century as it is today.

St. Augustine of Hippo

Although he was born in A.D. 354, St. Augustine of Hippo is still considered the greatest doctor of the Church, but he didn't get off to a very good start. His mother, named Monica or Monnica—we aren't quite sure which—was a pious Christian lady[1] who saw to it that Augustine went to Sunday School regularly, although they called it "catechumens" back then. When he finished the course, he wanted to be baptized a Christian, but Monica talked him out of it on the grounds that he probably would do some lusting and lurching after women and maybe a little drinking, too, while he was young and full of vinegar, and it would be a lot better if he waited until he ran out of gas a little and then got baptized so that the sins of his youth wouldn't go against his record.[2] So he waited, but by the time he had sown his wild oats, he was sort of out of the idea of being baptized and took a mistress instead.[3]

Augustine decided to be a college professor and a Manichean. He wanted to be a college professor because it was better than working, and he wanted to be a Manichean because all the intellectuals were joining.

As you must remember, the Manicheans believed that the world was not created by good old God but by another chap named God, who wasn't as good as good old God. They also insisted that Manicheans be celibate vegetarians, which cut down some on the number of converts to Manicheanism since not everyone wants to be a celibate vegetarian. After a while Augustine got tired of the Manicheans and became a skeptic.

He didn't like being a skeptic very well, either, so he be-

[1] She herself is a certified saint and her feast day is May 4. It isn't every day you get a mother and a son who are both genuine saints.

[2] Today many Christian Churches insist on baptism for adults only, but perhaps not for this reason.

[3] He was a firm believer in the doctrine that the way to happiness is through the mind and that bodily passions are to be rigidly suppressed—or at least that's what he said he believed.

came a Neo-Platonist. The Neo-Platonists had many dandy doctrines that the Manicheans had never even thought of such as the immateriality and the immortality of the soul, and that there is a sort of perfect spiritual world all about us, but though we have a built-in antenna to help us to tune in on it, you almost have to be a Neo-Platonist to get the message. Also, you didn't have to be a celibate vegetarian to be a Neo-Platonist. Augustine liked Neo-Platonism a lot and stuck with it. He claimed that it was exactly the same thing as Catholic Christianity, a statement that many Neo-Platonists didn't care for much.

Augustine's mother didn't mind if he was a Neo-Platonist or not, so long as he was a baptized Christian, which he wasn't. Good Christian woman that she was, she believed that bishops are smarter than anybody, so she asked her bishop to have a talk with Augustine and show him the error of his ways, whatever they were, and by reason and pious argument, get him converted. The bishop, though, knew that Augustine was an arguer rated well up in the heavyweight division and felt that he would be overmatched, so he told Monica that praying for Augustine would be better. At any rate, prayers and Neo-Platonism persuaded Augustine to be baptized, and there was no holding him after that, although when he wanted to make an honest woman of his mistress,[4] his mother said it would hurt his future career, talked him into just deserting her, and found him a wealthy fiancée as a replacement.[5]

Augustine was by now a fast-rising comet in the firmament

[4] They had a son by now. His name was Adeodatus.

[5] Scholars debate for hours at a time whether Augustine excelled his mother in piety and holiness or his mother excelled Augustine. The consensus seems to be that Monica had a little bit of an edge.

of the teaching profession and could look forward to a long and brilliant career. Not only were successful teachers popular public figures back then, but for the real stars of the profession there was quite a bit of dough in it. He decided, however, that if he was ever going to be a saint he would have to go off somewhere and think saintly thoughts. Since he was suffering from lung trouble, and also some friends had nickled up and provided a handsome fund to support him in his saintliness, he decided a career of saintly thinking would be the thing to do, if he only had a divine revelation that it would be the thing to do, which he got rather shortly. Since he was a new Christian, he spent a year at Rome to get the hang of it, then retired to his hometown which, as you undoubtedly remember, was Tagaste in Numidia, as an apprentice saint. He became a priest, and then only four years later was made bishop of Hippo Regius. He said he didn't want to be a bishop and only did it because everybody insisted. This attitude became the model for priests and clergymen who were made into bishops, and even today every new bishop is expected to say, in his acceptance speech, that he would rather be a parish pastor but that he is accepting the bishopric because everyone insists on it.

Augustine was a great believer in reason as the highest activity of man and the only way to find truth until he became a bishop. After that, he naturally was able to see that truth was best got at by accepting the authority of the bishop and letting him tell you what truth is.[6] Also, before becoming a Christian he said the only way to be happy was to be wise,

[6] He came to this view by his powers of reason, and it is a view still widely accepted in Christian circles, especially by bishops.

but after becoming a Christian, he said the only way to be happy was to be pious.[7]

As a bishop, Augustine liked persecuting heretics, but he wasn't very hard on them really, mostly confining himself to writing nasty things about them. He was especially good at giving hell to the Donatists and the Pelagians, and once even had some Donatists tossed in the clink for a while, but no one can blame him much for this because everyone knows what a nuisance Donatists can be. Also, he would take on his old buddies the Manichaens every now and then and prove conclusively that they were totally wrong about everything.

Mostly, though, Augustine is known as an idea man. We can't go into his ideas too much, although you should rest assured that they are sound.[8] Briefly though, he was the first to suspect that time is subjective rather than objective; he explained that the persons of the Holy Trinity are to be compared to memory, understanding, and will, rather than how Gregory of Nyssa compared them (Gregory of Nyssa said they were like Peter, James, and John); and he showed us that evil is just the tendency of created things to lapse into the nothingness from which they came, which has helped us a lot.

Where Augustine really shines, though, is in his thoughts on the foreknowledge of God and the freedom of man. Since God knows ahead of time everything that is going to happen to you, it has to happen that way and there isn't a damn thing you can do about it, he said. However, don't ever think that you aren't free, he said, because freedom isn't doing what

---

[7] Christians still value piety above wisdom.

[8] He interpreted reality in the genuinely Eleatic sense, which is a comfort to us.

Osborn

you want to do but is freedom from evil, and if God knows you are to be saved, you can't help being free from evil, and freedom from evil is what freedom really means. This led to the formulation of the famous doctrine of double predestination. Before Augustine it had been thought that God only predestines certain people to go to heaven and that in going to hell, you are on your own. Augustine saw clearly that God in His goodness predestines people both to heaven and to hell.[9] It is hard to see how we could have gotten along all these years without the doctrine of double predestination.

We mustn't forget that it was Augustine who gave us the clue to understanding history, which is that everything from the beginning of time is to be understood in the light of the Roman Catholic Church. The Roman Catholic Church, he explained, is the sole ark of salvation as well as the supreme authority on earth, which simplifies things no end.

The brilliance of Augustine's works on theology has obscured somewhat his contribution to science. The standard description of the world at the time was contained in *The Christian Topography* of Cosmos Indicopleustes, an Egyptian monk, which demonstrated that one need only look in the Bible and see from the dimensions of Noah's Ark and the Tabernacle of Moses that the world is a flat parallelogram surrounded by high walls supporting a cylindrical vault, and that all this is divided horizontally into three stories with hell below us and heaven above us.

Augustine held with Indicopleustes that, indeed, the Bible is the only possible source of accurate information about the natural universe, but that on rational and biblical grounds

[9] Augustine explained that the number of people predestined to go to heaven is eternally fixed, and equals exactly the number of fallen angels now in hell. He did not tell us what this number is.

anyone can plainly see that the earth is a sphere but that there can't possibly be anyone on the other side as they would have to walk with their heads pointing down instead of up, which is ridiculous. He condemned the study of astronomy because it seeks to nose around in secrets we weren't intended to know, and he felt the study of anatomy ought to be banned because it is a bloody business at best.

Historians claim that, more than any other man, Augustine helped the world make the transition from the spirit of classical antiquity to the spirit of the Middle Ages, which some people consider an improvement and some don't.

Having preached thousands of sermons and written many books, treatises, polemics, etc., plus innumerable letters,[10] and all the time being a bishop and pushing heretics around and doing other energy-consuming things, Augustine got tired in his seventy-sixth year and died, just as the Vandals were in the process of knocking off the Roman Empire. In fact, when he conked out on August 28, 430 A.D., the Vandals were just outside the walls of Hippo Regius, and it was obvious that they would soon be on the inside, which may have given Augustine the idea that this was as good a time to go as any.

The Lessons

St. Augustine's long and rather dull life is so rich in practical lessons for today's secular man that one hardly knows where to begin. However, for starters, let us observe that:

(a) A wealthy father may give a boy the best leg up on

[10] Considering how things get lost, and the fact that we have four hundred of Augustine's sermons and 217 of his letters preserved today, he must have turned out a truly staggering total.

success, but a pious, conniving mother is not to be sneezed at.

(b) It's O.K. to switch from being a Christian to a roué to a Manichean to a skeptic to a Neo-Platonist so long as you eventually settle on something and stick with it.

(c) If you talk all the time and write stuff by the bale, eventually some people are going to pay attention to you.

(d) For a dedicated career man it is better to have a rich fiancée than a poor mistress.

(e) If you want to be considered an authority by posterity, there is no field like theology because nobody can prove you are wrong, but you are well-advised to lay off science because posterity can check you out on science.

(f) Living a long life is dandy, but it is more important to pick the right time to die.

St. Catherine of Sweden

St. Catherine is a saint because she lived with her husband Count Eggard, "in continence and piety" for a while, then went home to live with her mother, St. Bridget.

The Lesson

Many wives go home to mother, but not all of them are saints.

St. Ludger

St. Ludger was bishop of Münster when Charlemagne was King, and one day he had an appointment with the King but kept the King waiting while he finished saying his breviary. This made Charlemagne mad and he gave Ludger hell, but Ludger said, "King, when you appointed me bishop you said I should put the service of God ahead of service to the King, didn't you?"

"I did at that," the King said, and got over being mad at St. Ludger.

The Lesson

When you keep the boss waiting, you'd better have a good excuse.

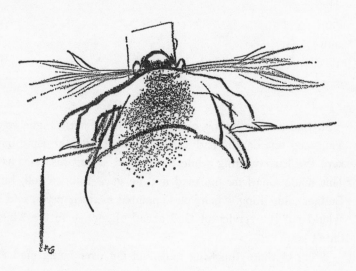

St. Theodosius the Cenobite

Theodosius was born about 425 at Garissus in Cappadocia, not that it makes any difference. As a young man he decided to try for sainthood. In those days the vocation of sainthood was pretty much restricted to monks, hermits, and ecclesiastics who led rather austere lives. But even in the fifth century, an aspirant for canonization could opt for either the eremitic or the cenobitic[1] life. Theodosius agonized over this formidable decision, but finally chose to be a cenobite. Historians are agreed that it was a wise choice because Theodosius turned out to be a ball of fire as a cenobite.

He began in a small way. Finding some empty caves in the suburbs of Jerusalem, he set up in business there[2] with but a handful of followers. Theodosius realized that if his modest little monastery was to become the great big, booming, successful monastery he intended it to be, he would have to have some publicity. So he passed a rule of the house that all his followers were to meditate ceaselessly on death. Since this isn't easy unless you have a morbid turn of mind, he dug a grave and worked out a schedule for each of his cenobites to spend a portion of every day sitting by the open grave thinking unpleasant thoughts.

His plan was an instant success. It got people to talking, and they came from everywhere to see the Theodosians sitting by a hole in the ground. You and I would never have thought of this, but then, you have to remember that they didn't have television back then. Soon his caves were crammed with cenobites, many of whom had forsaken less exciting monastic communities to join up with Theodosius, and he had long waiting lists of applicants.

So Theodosius did what any good businessman would have

[1] An eremite had to go it alone, while a cenobite was permitted to endure the miseries of mortal existence in the company of his saintly chums.

[2] The caves were rent-free, thus greatly reducing the overhead.

done: He expanded. He leased his caves to a small cenobitic outfit just getting started,[3] and built a new plant.

Market research demonstrated conclusively that Cathismus, a bustling little place near Bethlehem, was the ideal location for the sort of operation he had in mind. Then "he raised an immense monastery which finally sheltered a host of cenobites." His biographers do not specify how many is a "host," but we can assume that it is a lot of cenobites. The new plant contained three infirmaries for various classes of ailments and four churches. Three of the churches were reserved respectively for Greeks, Germans, and Slavs where they could pray in their own language. In the fourth it was O.K. to pray in any old language.

The phenomenal growth of the Theodosians naturally aroused jealousy among competitors. They got to the politicians, and when Theodosius was about ninety, the Emperor Anastasius, who was known as the protector of the Eutychians,[4] condemned him to exile.[5] But the Emperor wasn't long for this world, and after his death, Theodosius returned to Cathismus and spent the rest of his life running his monastery, where he died full of years (105 to be exact) and infirmities.[6]

[3] After filling up the open grave. He didn't want the competition doing his thing.

[4] The Eutychians, a rival cenobitic company, were tired of being no. 2.

[5] A primitive form of anti-trust judgment.

[6] Brought on, perhaps, by his vegetarian diet. He ate only vegetables and fruits, and his biographers record that he passed thirty years without eating a morsel of bread. He tried to promote vegetarianism as the correct Christian diet, but it never caught on.

The Lessons

The life of Theodosius the Cenobite stands by itself, and the lessons to be learned from it are so apparent as to require no elaboration. Let us set down two or three, however, just in case you have overlooked them:

(a) If you want to make it big, you need a gimmick.

(b) The life of a cenobite doesn't sound like fun, but it is probably more fun than being an eremite.

(c) Never forget that nothing succeeds like success, in sainthood or anything else.

St. Leobardus

St. Leobardus was supposed to get married, but as the wedding day approached, he chickened out and just took off for parts unknown. He finally settled down at Marmoutier, where he hacked a small room in a big rock and spent the rest of his life there reading *The Lives of the Fathers* and copying the Psalms on old pieces of parchment somebody gave him.

The Lesson

Marriage may be no bed of roses, but it is undoubtedly preferable to sleeping in a rock.

St. Humbert

Humbert, who lived in the seventh century, became a priest at an early age, but he had to give it up when his parents died because he inherited such a large fortune that it was a full-time job to look after it. However, he gave a bundle to the Monastery of Maroilles on the Hespres, and for his generosity he was made a saint.

The Lessons

(a) If you don't have time for good works, making money is the next best thing.

(b) Bestowing a large cash gift on an institution could get you an honorary degree back in the seventh century, and it still can.

St. Josaphat

Born in Poland, St. Josaphat was baptized and brought up in the Orthodox Ruthenian Church. When he was sixteen years old, the Ruthenian Church united with the Roman Church, and he entered the Basilian Monastery of the Trinity at Vilna.

It was at this time that he changed his name from Kuircevey to Josaphat.[1] The monastery had only one monk, an archimandrite named Samuel. Samuel was the father superior, and he loudly proclaimed loyalty to the Pope. What else could he say? But Josaphat cleverly saw that behind Samuel's professed loyalty to the Pope lurked a secret attachment to Orthodoxy[2]—and courageously exposed him for the heretic he was. The bishop deposed Samuel and after carefully considering the situation, he elevated Josaphat to the post of father superior.

Josaphat, from that time forth, never preached a sermon without proclaiming *his* fidelity to the Pope. But after a while the Cossacks decided that Orthodox was orthodox instead of heretical and threw Josaphat out.

Josaphat went on preaching that the Pope was the only true successor to St. Peter, and the people beat him to death with sticks.

The Lessons

(a) Having one big idea has something to be said for it, but sooner or later you are likely to become a bore.

(b) It is clever to undermine the boss when you are in a position to get his job, but remember to keep an eye on the guy who is next in line below you.

(c) Hunting heretics is an ancient and still popular enter-

[1] Wouldn't you?

[2] Orthodoxy spelled with a capital O. When spelled with a capital O, Orthodoxy is a dirty word to a papist. When spelled with a small o, papists are all for it.

prise, but once you start a heresy hunt, you can't be sure the hunters won't bag you.

Blessed Louise of Savoy

Blessed Louise was the daughter of Blessed Amadeus, as well as the granddaughter of Charles VII and a niece of Louis XI. She lived a happy life with her husband, Hugh of Chalons.

The Lesson

One can get to be a saint by suffering, self-denial, rigid virtue, and other strenuous practices, but good connections will do just as well.

St. Athanasius

Very few saints are so widely remembered today as Athanasius. This is because he spent a rather long life combating Arianism.[1] He became bishop of Alexandria in 328 when he

[1] The Arians insisted that in defining Christological doctrine, one word in the formula should read "homoiuosious." Athanasius maintained that it should be "homouosious." It seemed important at the time.

was only thirty-three years of age. Every so often the admiring faithful would gather around the episcopal palace and chant, "He is a good man and an excellent Christian; he is an ascetic and a true bishop."[2] Athanasius was bishop for forty-five years, but he spent twenty-two of these forty-five years in exile. Whenever the Arians could get next to the Emperor, they would talk him into replacing Athanasius with a bishop of sound Arian principles.[3] He was exiled a total of six times. It got so that whenever he was exiled, he bought a round-trip ticket. During these periods of disfavor, the Arians would say nasty things about him,[4] but Athanasius used these enforced vacations to catch up on his writings, which included notable works of exegesis, doctrinal letters, a life of St. Anthony of Thebaid, and several personal apologia. These last are said to be very bitter in tone, but then, if you'd been exiled six times, you'd be bitter, too.

Athanasius is best remembered today as the author of the Athanasian Creed, which he didn't write.

The Lessons

The life of St. Athanasius teaches us that

(a) It is great to become a member of the establishment before you are forty, but life at the top can be rocky.

[2] It sounds better in Latin.

[3] Once his replacement was Gregory of Cappadocia, and another time, George of Cappadocia. Cappadocia was not Athanasius' favorite city.

[4] Once they said that he had assassinated Bishop Arsenius of Ypsele after first cutting off the bishop's hand, but this was never proved.

(b) Doctrinal purity is awfully nice, but it hardly seems worth six exiles.

(c) If you want to be remembered for seventeen hundred years, it is less important to do something outstanding than it is to get your name attached to it.

Sts. Cyriacus, Largus, Smaragdus, and Sirinnius

These four noble Romans were very generous in helping the poor Christians forced to help build the palace and the baths for Emperor Diocletian. The authorities said that this was illegal, put them in prison, and later executed them.

The Lesson

Charity is among the greatest of Christian virtues, but you should make sure it is tax-deductible.

St. Medard

St. Medard never did anything of a world-shaking nature except invest Queen Radegunde with the deaconess's habit when she got fed up with King Clotaire and entered a convent, but he is one of the best-remembered and most popular saints in rural France because someone thought up the religious feast of the Rose Queen, an annual ceremony in the churches of France at which a local girl "who has most edified the parish" during the last twelve months is crowned with

roses, and Medard took the credit for it, and because the
farmers say

> Should St. Medard's day be wet
> It will rain for forty yet;
> At least until St. Barnabas
> The summer sun won't favor us.

The Lesson

St. Medard's life calls our attention to a fundamental
principle for successful living. It is this: If you don't have any
talent, what you need is a good press agent.

St. Aloysius Gonzaga

Aloysius' mother wanted him to be a churchman, and his
father, who was a marquis or something equally impressive,
wanted him to be a soldier. His father had the first shot at it,
dressing up little Aloysius, who was four years old at the time,
in soldier clothes and sending him to hang around with the
troops the old man was raising for the King of Spain. About
the only discernible influence this had on Aloysius was that at
the age of four he learned to swear like a trooper. He later
referred to this period in his life as his "life of sin," and he
never forgave himself for it.

In 1577 his father sent him to the Medici Court in Florence, because he thought that if anyone could knock the piety out of Aloysius, the Medicis could. This didn't work, either, for Aloysius, while there, pronounced a vow of perpetual chastity[1] and learned to meditate an hour at a stretch without his mind wandering.

In 1585 he followed his mother's wishes and became a monk and went in for strange mortifications, including refusing to look at his mother's face.[2] The only recorded wisdom from his lips reads as follows:

"We have no right to pride ourselves on our birth; the great are dust like the poor; perhaps their dust stinks even worse, and that is all."

The Lessons

(a) If you want to learn to cuss fluently, the quickest way is to join the army.

(b) Women may be the weaker sex, but they usually get their way in the end.

(c) To win a permanent place in the hearts of posterity, it is unnecessary to say very much so long as what you say is sufficiently profound.

Sts. Bertha and Gumbert

Bertha and Gumbert were man and wife, but they evidently didn't get along too well, so they decided to break it up and go

---

[1] Very unusual for anyone at a Medici Court.
[2] This may be significant. Then again, it may not.

it alone. Gumbert went off to convert Ireland, but the Irish didn't particularly appreciate his efforts and beheaded him or something. Bertha became the abbess of a convent, but her nephews killed her because she was giving all her money away to the Church.

The Lesson

A marriage can be pretty bad at times, but the alternatives may be worse.

St. Peter Paschal of Granada

St. Peter Paschal was named bishop of Jain, but he wasn't bishop long before King Mouley Mohammed of Granada chopped his head off.

The Lesson

Making it to the top is sometimes easier than staying there.

St. Jerome

You remember St. Jerome because he was the one who translated the Bible into Latin, which wasn't easy. It took him thirty years. This monumental work is called "The Vulgate," which, I suppose, is as good a name for it as any. What you don't know is that he did far more interesting things than translate the Bible into Latin.

For example, his biographers tell us that before he was baptized, his conduct "left something to be desired." They don't tell us exactly what he did, but we can imagine. He came from a rich family, so he could afford about any kind of sin which appealed to him. Then, after he became a priest he went to Rome and was secretary to the Pope, but he was still having a high old time, or so it was said. He was given charge of the religious instruction of a group of patrician ladies, among them three named Marcella, Paula, and Eustochium with whom he was especially chummy. He liked Paula best, though, which is no mystery, as we shall see in a moment. There was so much talk that he had to proclaim that nothing irregular was going on,[1] but he thought it best to get out of town. In fact, he got out of Europe and went to live in Bethlehem in a monastery Paula had built for him. From this point on he settled down to the business of piety and scholarship. After all, he was around forty by this time, and back in the fourth century forty was pretty old.

[1] What did you expect him to say?

We don't have any records of how he did at piety, but he was certainly a whiz-bang at scholarship. In addition to translating the Bible, he also translated the works of Origen, wrote several biographies, exegetics, histories, polemic, and batches of letters. His works take up six thousand columns in Migne's *Patrology*, which ought to impress you quite a bit. As late as 1920 Pope Benedict XV said that St. Jerome had been given to the Church by heaven itself and was still its greatest doctor, which is a dandy tribute to Jerome's staying power as a saint.

The Lessons

We all appreciate St. Jerome's efforts at translating the Bible into Latin, but we also appreciate the fine practical lessons we are able to extract from his example, which are:

(a) The rich probably don't sin any more than the poor, but the rich have a wider choice of sins.

(b) It may be true that while sticks and stones will break your bones, words will never hurt you, but if there is enough racy gossip going round about you, it is wise to locate in a new community.

(c) If you are so fortunate as to have a choice of girl friends, pick the one who can build you a house.

St. Florentina

Our information about the life of St. Florentina is very sketchy. We know that she had three brothers who are saints (St. Leander, St. Fulgentius [bishop of Ecija], and St. Isidore of Seville are who they were), and her mother's name was Turtur, which means turtledove. We don't know her father's name.[1] She got to be a saint for a rather unusual reason, which is a long and flowery letter written to her by her brother, St. Leander, in which he recounts her saintly qualities,[2] and which she managed to save and pass on to posterity. She is buried in the Cathedral of Seville alongside St. Leander.

The Lesson

Save those old letters. You never can tell when one of them might come in handy.

[1] We assume that her mother knew it, though.

[2] Among other things, he says that there is nothing in all creation worthy of her; that virginity is a state so ineffable that it is impossible to say enough good things about it; and that he groans at the thought that somehow she might lose it.

St. Raymund of Pennafort

St. Raymund, who was born in 1175, was a teacher of philosophy at the age of twenty, and earned his doctorate not much later, so we know that he was pretty smart. The Pope wanted him to be one of the top dogs in the Church, a vicar general or archbishop or something equally prestigious and remunerative, but Raymund wanted to expiate his sins instead, so the Pope said he could be an ordinary Dominican friar—not a bad job for a chap whose chief ambition is to expiate his sins.

One would think that Raymund had compiled an impressive list of sins since he was so hung up on expiating them, but he had been so busy getting his Ph.D. that he really hadn't had the time to do anything very lurid, and it turns out that all he was feeling guilty about was that he was a little strong-minded and also had noticed in himself a faint tendency toward spiritual pride. You and I would think that a couple of Hail Marys and perhaps a pater noster would take care of the situation nicely, but not Raymund. He begged his superiors to sock it to him in the form of some whopping penance, so they told him to go write a book on moral theology, which gives you an idea of the Dominican concept of suffering in the thirteenth century but which Raymund considered wouldn't expiate anything more than an impure thought of negligible horsepower or a mild cussword or two. He wrote it, though, and the book was a big critical, though not commercial, success.

Raymund was noted for being kind, compassionate, of a loving disposition, and for whipping up the Kingdom of Aragon to a holy war against the Mohammedans.[1] He also was a high-octane preacher against the bodily passions, and in three years collected in five volumes all the decrees of the Popes since the last collection of Gratian in 1150. Thus, he covered a period of eighty-four years of papal decrees, and since all Popes are fond of rendering decrees, the only surprising thing is that five volumes would hold them all. These are known as *The Decretals*, and are indispensable to Vatican lawyers, although a breathless and expectant world had to wait until 1916 for a complete collection of *The Decretals*. Another of Raymund's contributions to mankind was compulsory retirement at age sixty-five.[2]

Having earlier disposed of the Mohammedans, Raymund decided to take out after the Saracens, but this time instead of a war he got St. Thomas Aquinas to write *The Summa Contra Gentiles* for the Saracens to read, which is almost as bad as a war.

As a part of his crusade to convert the infidels, he went to the island of Majorca where the King had several wives, and he told the King to give up all but one, which the King said he would be glad to do as soon as he could figure out a way to

[1] One biographer notes that Raymund entered into the work of promoting this holy war "with great zeal and charity." If you wonder how one goes about starting a war in the spirit of charity, you must remember that professional theologians like Raymund understand some things that are beyond the layman's grasp.

[2] This came about because he was General of the Order of St. Dominic and was sick and tired of the job, so he decreed that the General of the Order had to retire when he reached retirement age, which Raymund set at sixty-five because he happened to be sixty-five at the time.

tell them to go home. Since the King didn't seem to be in any hurry to get on with it, Raymund said he was leaving as it offended him to associate with a man with more than one wife, but the King said he couldn't go. "The hell I can't," Raymund said,[3] then spread his cape on the surface of the sea, tied up one corner of it to his staff so as to make a sail, stepped on it, and shot off toward Barcelona. He arrived in Barcelona six hours later which, since it is a distance of 180 miles, was an average of thirty miles per hour, a record at the time and seldom bettered since then. When he beached his cape-boat he gathered it up and put it on, as it was dry, and went off to a monastery to spend his remaining days in penance, in prayer, and in preparation for his passage to eternity. A little later he fell ill and died an untimely death at the age of one hundred.

The Lessons

St. Raymund of Pennafort is one of the most likable of saints, and his unusually edifying life helps us to see that:

(a) All of us probably suffer from guilt feelings, but the sins that bug you may not bother me at all.

(b) Do not be too quick to condemn a war because it may have been started in all Christian charity.

(c) If you plan a trip abroad but the ships are booked solid, remember that you don't have to go by boat.

[3] What he actually said was, "A King of the earth endeavors to deprive us of the means of retiring, but the King of Heaven will supply us with the means," but this is just how theologians talk when they mean "the hell I can't."

St. Meinrad of Swabia

St. Meinrad lived for a while on one of the peaks of Mt. Etzel, but later he went off to live in the depths of the forest of Sihl, where some bandits, who thought he had a hidden treasure, killed him.

The Lesson

If you act secretive, don't be surprised if people think you have a secret.

St. John Joseph of the Cross[1]

John Joseph Calosirto was one of five brothers who became monks so it must have run in the family, although a family can die out pretty fast if all the boys enter the celibate life. At the age of sixteen he entered the order of friars minor of the Alcantarine Reform at Naples and zipped right to the top in

---

[1] Commonly known as St. John of the Cross. Not to be confused with St. John Chrysostom, St. John Climacus, St. John before the Latin Gate, Blessed John of Parma, Blessed John of Penna, Blessed John Nelson, or fifty to sixty other saint and blessed Johns.

the Alcantarine Reform, becoming guardian, definitor, and provincial of the order, or in other words the boss, before he was thirty.

But he got tired of this heady existence as a big-shot executive, and resigned to devote his life to mortification, mysticism, and miracles, the three M's of sainthood achievable only by the super-pious. He did awfully well at all three.

In mortification he managed to catch something which covered his whole body with sores, and he prevented them from healing by picking at them all the time, a practice we find disgusting in people who don't know any better, but which is commendable and praiseworthy in someone who is doing it as a means of salvation and a rung on the difficult ladder to sainthood. This would have been adequate mortification for most saints, but for John of the Cross it was only good for openers. He wore sandals which bristled with sharp nails, and he had a cross a foot long with a lot of big spikes in it which he wore next to his skin with the spikes down. Also, he never raised his eyes, he slept sitting on the ground, wouldn't listen to music, and went thirty years without a drink, the last item of which strikes us as excessive mortification even for a saint of John's stature.

He was almost as good at miracles as he was at mortification. Sometimes he would transfer a bad case of stomach ulcers from the sufferer to himself, as if he didn't have enough aches and pains already. He also foretold the future, read the secrets of hearts, and, we are told, was "constantly ravished in ecstasy."[2] He also was, and presumably still is, especially

[2] The author is a little hazy as to what it is to be constantly ravished in ecstasy, but it sounds like more fun than wearing a spiked cross.

Osborn

good at miracles of bilocation and levitation, which, as everyone knows, are among the most difficult of miracles to
perform.

His reputation as a mystic rests on his still-popular book
titled *The Dark Night of the Soul,* the thesis of which is that
there are times when even a saint doesn't feel so good, or at
least there were times when he didn't, which, considering his
habits of life, isn't surprising.

The Lessons

The life of St. John Joseph of the Cross may not inspire many of us to emulate him, but at least it teaches us that:

(a) The life of a top-echelon executive no doubt has its problems, but other vocations have their problems, too.

(b) Mortification of the flesh may well be one way to achieve salvation, but it occasionally makes you out of sorts.

(c) It is a heroic thing to go thirty years without a drink, but a little snort now and then will make you feel lots better.

Blessed Eve of Liège

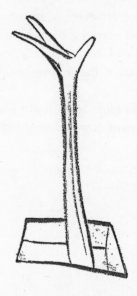

Blessed Eve lived her whole saintly life as a recluse, and that is all we know about her except that she came to the attention of those who process candidates for sainthood because of her close friendship with the famous St. Juliana.[1]

[1] This was St. Juliana of Cornillon, not St. Juliana of Nicomedia or St. Juliana Falconieri, as you might have thought at first glance. Juliana Falconieri is mainly remembered as the niece of St. Alexis, and Juliana of Nicomedia wouldn't be remembered at all if she hadn't refused to marry the prefect of Nicomedia and gotten herself beheaded, so Juliana of Cornillon, who founded the feast of Corpus Christi, is clearly the class of the Julianas.

The Lesson

In sainthood, as in other vocations, it's not what you know but who you know that counts.

St. Sebastian

St. Sebastian is chiefly remembered today because practically all Renaissance artists painted pictures of him so full of arrows that he looked like a porcupine. This came about due to the fact that Sebastian had become a soldier inasmuch as he thought nobody would suspect that he was a Christian if he enlisted in the army of the Emperor Diocletian, as this was not considered a Christian thing to do. But Diocletian caught on and turned him over to the archers who shot him up pretty good and thought he was dead, but he wasn't.[1]

When Sebastian recovered he decided to try a different tack, so he went to see Diocletian to try to persuade him to go easy on the Christians. He felt certain that the Emperor would listen to reason and kindly arguments, but the Emperor didn't and turned Sebastian over to the soldiers again and told them this time to finish the job, which they did, beating Sebastian to death with cudgels and throwing him in a sewer.

[1] The Romans were excellent soldiers, but they never quite got the hang of the bow and arrow.

The Lesson

Reason and sweet talk works with most people, but it works better with Emperors if you have an army to back you up.

St. Pulcheria

Pulcheria, Empress of the Eastern Empire, forced her younger brother Theodosius II to marry the daughter of a pagan philosopher, forced the girl to become a Christian, and bossed her around all the time. She twisted arms at the Council of Chalcedon and got it to condemn Eutychianism. She took a vow of perpetual virginity, but married General Marcian, a handsome and virile soldier eight years younger than she was. The Pope said of her: "Thanks to you the whole earth is at present united in a same confession of the truth."

The Lesson

Very few saints had as few saintly qualities as St. Pulcheria, which indelibly impresses us with the fact that if you aren't qualified for an honor, plenty of political clout will make up for your deficiencies.

St. Canute

When Sueno II,[1] Christian King of Denmark died, he left no legal heirs to the throne, but he did have quite a number of illegitimate children, among whom was Canute. Canute didn't succeed to the throne right off, though, because his bastard brother Harold the Idle beat him to it. Harold the Idle didn't last long, though, and Canute succeeded him.

Canute tried to do good, like a Christian King should, and instituted reforms and set an example of personal virtue for the people and demonstrated a commendable zeal for the conversion of his subjects, all of which was greatly appreciated by the people. They thought Canute was a big improvement over Harold the Idle.

When he had gotten things going pretty well at home, Canute decided it was time to start a war somewhere,[2] and he picked England because it was rather convenient to Denmark. But William the Conqueror knocked him off quite easily, leaving Denmark with a big bill and no conquered territory to tax, so Canute had to raise taxes in Denmark. Canute's loyal and loving subjects then revolted and, finding Canute one day in church, proceeded to hack him to pieces.

[1] My editor, who has a thing about the Vikings, claims this should be Swain, but, of course, I must stick to what they call him in the authorized hagiographies.

[2] Someone told him it was his Christian duty.

The Lesson

The life of St. Canute is particularly helpful for aspiring politicians because it shows that while people like their Kings and Presidents and other leaders to be virtuous and religious and to institute sound programs of reform, they like low taxes better.

St. Alphonsus Liguori

St. Alphonsus started out as a lawyer, but he lost a case and decided to become a priest. As a priest, he wrote a lot of stuff[1] and suffered many temptations and trials. He died in disgrace.

[1] His best-known work was a book on moral theology which extolled the system of "probabilism," which, as you know, is sort of halfway between the position of the rigourists and the position of the laxists.

The Lesson

Failure at a secular profession may constitute a divine call to the ministry, but you can't be sure.

St. Anthony of the Desert

St. Anthony was born in A.D. 250 in Heracleus, which, as you probably know, is in upper Egypt. He started out being a saint by living in an old sepulcher, but he found that he had to fight all the time with the demons who lived there too.

After a while he went out into the desert and found an abandoned fort which he liked better and moved in there. Word
got around, and flocks of people came out to admire him and
his home in the fort—so many, in fact, that he had to build
two monasteries to hold all those who wanted to be saints in
the desert. One monastery was on the right bank of the Nile
at Pispir, and the other was on the left bank at Arsinoe.

St. Anthony never did anything especially exciting, except
for a few days in A.D. 311 when he went to Alexandria to
combat the Arian heresy, but he soon went back to his fort in
the desert. He lived to be 105 years old, and is today one of
our better-known saints[1] because St. Athanasius wrote *The
Life of St. Anthony of the Desert,* which is said to have had a
profound influence both on art and hagiography.

The Lessons

For a saint who lived a long and uncommonly uneventful
life, St. Anthony of the Desert offers us a whopping number
of useful lessons, some of which are:

(a) When looking for a quaint old place to remodel, an

---

[1] He is known as "the Father of the Cenobites," which is quite
an honor.

abandoned fort has more possibilities than an old
sepulcher.

(b) If you build a better monastery, the world will beat a
path to your door.

(c) Relaxing in the desert is a fine formula for longevity,
but there isn't much to do out there.

(d) Your life can have a profound influence on art and
hagiography and almost anything you care to name
without any strenuous effort on your part so long as
you have a first-rate biographer.

St. Dismas

Dismas[1] was a thief, but because he happened to be hung
alongside Christ and because he reprimanded the other thief
hanging with him for showing a bad disposition, he has gone
down in Christian history as "the good thief," and has been
made a saint.

The Lesson

If you are a crook, sometimes it pays off to get caught, but
not often.

[1] We aren't sure his name was Dismas, but we are sure he was
a thief.

St. Simeon Stylites

Among saints who have gotten to be saints by spectacular methods, St. Simeon Stylites is surely in the first rank if not the champion, but you would never have guessed he was going to make it big in the saint business if you had seen him as a young boy, because he was nothing but an ignorant sheepherder.

What happened was that while herding sheep one day he heard a voice say, "Woe upon you who laugh now; you shall mourn and weep." No doubt he immediately recognized this as Luke, Chapter VI, Verse 25, but since he didn't have a Bible commentary handy, he asked an old man what it meant. The old man replied that as he was old and full of wisdom and experience, he could state with little fear of contradiction that it meant if you want eternal happiness the best thing to do is to suffer, and that suffering in solitude is practically 100 percent guaranteed to produce eternal happiness.

So Simeon left his sheep and joined up with some hermits to practice suffering and mortification. He wasn't doing too well at it until he hit on the idea of having himself walled up in a cell on Ash Wednesday and staying there without food or water until Easter Sunday.[1] This worked like a charm, because people came from everywhere to see the walled-up room with Simeon inside, and had picnics around the place

[1] This is forty days, not counting Sundays, in case you had forgotten.

and in general made a mess, and were noisy and not very pious.

Simeon discovered that he couldn't meditate and pray very well with all that racket going on, and besides the idea was to suffer in solitude. So he had someone build a tall column and he climbed up to the top of it, and spent the rest of his life there, which was several years. He stood up all the time, as there wasn't room to sit down, and since it wasn't enclosed or anything, he got pretty wet and cold sometimes, which is as good a way to suffer as any.

Sometimes he would preach sermons to the people who came to gawk at him,[2] and he counseled people who asked him to solve their personal problems.[3] He also worked a miracle every now and then.

When he was sixty-nine years old he finally came down off his pillar because as he was bowing for his first prayer of the day he toppled off, and that was the end of Simeon Stylites.

The Lessons

The life of Simeon Stylites surely excites the imagination and sends it racing off in quest of practical lessons. Two of the ones which are easy to track down are:

(a) When you need advice it isn't always a good idea to ask the first old man you see.

(b) Spending your life standing on top of a pillar is a great

[2] He preached on feast days, after nones. Since every day or so is some kind of a feast day, that is a lot of sermons.

[3] If he dealt with many marital problems, this must have been fun for the crowds hanging around his pillar.

way to suffer, but the plumbing facilities leave something to be desired.

St. Simeon Stylites the Younger[1]

St. Simeon Stylites the Younger sat for sixty-five years on pointed rocks and worked a lot of miracles.

The Lesson

The example of this exceptionally holy man teaches us that sitting on pointed rocks for sixty-five years will get you a certain amount of attention, but it is a good idea to have something else going for you, too.

St. John before the Latin Gate

St. Jerome, an authority of some reputation, tells us that in the year 95 John was arrested by Domitian.[2] He was brought

---

[1] Not to be confused with Simeon of Jerusalem, Simeon of Mantua, Simeon of Seleucia, Simeon of Trier, or Simeon Stylites.

[2] Emperor, an unsavory character from the Christian point of view.

to Rome and, near the gate leading to the Latium, was tossed
into a tub of boiling water. He emerged from this boiling bath
without so much as a singed hair.

The Lesson

From an exhaustive study of the life of St. John before the
Latin Gate, only one important lesson is to be distilled, but its
value is great indeed. It is this: Anyone can get into hot water.
The big thing is getting out unscalded.

Book Two

The Stalwart Christians

The Heroes We Cannot Neglect

It is necessary to divide our study of that splendid band of Christian heroes who have inspired emulation, devotion, and many other exemplary and desirable reactions in the lesser faithful into two sections: the saints and the noncanonized Stalwart Christians. This is because, although there is by no means a shortage of officially designated saints and in fact the Roman Church is still turning them out (though not as rapidly as it once did), there remains, after every bona fide saint is counted and numbered, a staggering supply of Christian heroes left over who can be neglected only to our loss.

Thousands of these leftovers are Roman Catholics, faithful and true, and in some cases with records of mortifications more gruesome than St. John of the Cross, or sufferers of indignities at the hands of heartless pagans more painful if not so spectacular as St. Sebastian.[1] One is moved to speculate on why, when so many have obviously been called, so few, relatively speaking, are chosen. Why, for example, was Clement of Alexandria denied canonization when Clement of Rome seemed to have no trouble at all grabbing off the prize? After all, C. of A. wrote the *Protrepticus* and the *Stromateis* and would have written the *Didascalos* except that unfortunately he died before he got around to it, while C. of R. is a misty figure whose very existence is in some doubt, and the only writing attributed to him is nothing to send the blood

[1] He was the one you see in all those paintings with arrows sticking out of him. See his biography in the section on the saints.

racing.[2] We are baffled by the neglect of Origen, who devised and perfected the system of deductive logic as applied to the discipline of theology while St. Mechtilde, whose only claim to holy eminence is that she lived in the same convent with St. Gertrude,[3] is safely stashed away in the pantheon of saints. There is a pious mystery here, but its unraveling is so formidable as to defy the powers of any but one who has the inside poop from the Vatican or is hep to the Byzantine ways of canonical councils.

The majority of these heroes of the faith who never made the grade as saints, though, have no reason whatever to slink around the lesser suburbs of heaven or hide their faces in shame from the cherubim and seraphim, or even St. Michael the Archangel for that matter. They missed the blessed accolade for the good and simple reason that they were Protestant Christians and, of course, Protestant Christians deplore the whole business of saints, except the original apostles and St. Paul and a few others who got in their licks very early in Christian history. Indeed, Martin Luther and John Calvin did no little bit to undermine the cult of saints, but they are Christian heroes of the top quality and if Protestants went in for manufacturing saints, would undoubtedly be listed in hagiographies as St. Martin of Wittenberg or St. John of Geneva.

Therefore, the author, for purposes of clarity, has designated these uncanonized but revered figures of holy history simply as Stalwart Christians.

[2] Some people say that Clement of Alexandria was rejected because he was a dirty intellectual, but we doubt that he was all that bad.

[3] St. Gertrude of Eisleben. Not to be confused with St. Gertrude of Nivelles or St. Gertrude Van der Oosten.

The reader will immediately notice two differences between our biographies of the saints and those of the Stalwart Christians.

The first difference is that the biographies of the Stalwart Christians are considerably longer than the biographies of the saints. This is not because we deem the Stalwart Christians more worthy of the space available than the saints. Nothing of the sort. It is only because the Stalwart Christians, who come along later in history than the saints we have selected, have had much more written about them so we know more about them. You can't write a great deal about St. Emmerick, whose total biography reads "Son of St. Stephen, King of Hungary." Nor does the available information on St. Sidonius, which consists of "a native of Ireland, became a monk at Jumièges and founded an abbey in Caux (d. about 689)," give a biographer much to go on. On the other hand, all the stuff written by and about Martin Luther overflows the library shelves, and the information on John Calvin, while not so voluminous as that on Luther, is still enough to break the back of a fair-sized elephant.

The second difference is that we do not draw the secular lessons from the lives of the Stalwart Christians and append them at the conclusion as we do for the saints. This is not because there are no lessons to be drawn, but because there are, in fact, too many of them to be drawn from the lives of the Stalwart Christians, and to attempt to filter them out and write them all down would make this volume—intended as it is for a place on the nightstand beside your bed and an easily portable companion which can be referred to daily—of prohibitive length and bulk. However, at the end of this section we shall include a chapter analyzing and summing up the secular wisdom which can be excavated from the lives and examples of the Stalwart Christians. Furthermore, since you have already worked your way through the lives of the saints, by now you have undoubtedly caught on to how to lift out these lessons for yourself, and so you are ready to launch into the Stalwart Christians entirely on your own.

Martin Luther

The sixteenth century was a God-awful age. People were superstitious, hostile to other nations and nationalities, Jews were persecuted, politicians were corrupt, Kings and nobles and even the upper middle class males kept mistresses, the poor resented the rich and frequently rioted against them, and the rich couldn't understand why the poor were discontented, and there were wars going on all the time, not to mention several other bad things.[1]

Martin Luther changed all this. He became the Father of the Protestant Reformation,[2] although he didn't intend to. What he intended to do was to save himself from the everlasting, nonconsuming flames of hell.[3] Everybody in the sixteenth century was trying to do the same thing, of course. To escape the clutches of the devil was supposed to be the chief end of man and the main motivation for human conduct. Actually, in theory the idea was to get oneself to heaven. But it was soon discovered that people weren't terribly enthusiastic about getting to heaven, so the Church shifted the emphasis to helping people avoid going to hell. This worked much better. You did this through being baptized, doing penance, performing good works, and accepting whatever the Church taught, no matter how nutty.

[1] The sixteenth century is also known as the Age of Faith.

[2] Reformations do not require mothers.

[3] Theologians are agreed that, though nonconsuming, they hurt every bit as much as conventional flames.

Martin Luther started life as the best kind of sixteenth-century Roman Catholic there was. The Church taught that children should obey their parents, so when Hans Luther, Martin's father, said to Martin, "You be a lawyer," fetching him a sharp clout to the chops for emphasis, Martin said "Yes, sir," and went off to study law.

To study law, he had to get into a university, and to get into a university, he had first to learn Latin and grammar and other dull subjects, which he did at schools in Mansfield, Magdeburg, and Eisenach.[4] He was then considered fit to be a college freshman, and matriculated at the University of Erfurt in May of 1501.[5] He was eighteen years old, which is about right for a college freshman. At Erfurt, as you know, the faculty was addicted to the nominalistic scholastic methodology, so Martin studied the syllogistic method and the categorical propositions of Petrus Hispanus.[6] It took him only a year to get his bachelor's degree, and three more years to get his master's degree. When he was awarded the master's, he said, "What grandeur and splendor to receive the master's. I think that no earthly joy can be compared to this."[7]

On July 2, 1505, Martin was returning home from a visit to some of his old buddies at Mansfield when en route he was overtaken by a sudden thunderstorm.[8] A bolt of lightning hit

[4] This isn't too important except that it shows what a nuisance it was to become an educated man in the sixteenth century.

[5] The university registered him as "Martinus Ludher ex Mansfelt." They were pretty hung up on Latin back then.

[6] Some of his detractors said he also studied the beer and the brothels of Erfurt a good bit, but their evidence is rather flimsy.

[7] This is how they talked in the sixteenth century when they meant, "Jeez, I'm glad that's over."

[8] He had gotten about to the town of Stotternheim when this happened; otherwise, you would never have heard of Stotternheim.

him and knocked him down. He wasn't hurt, but it scared the bejesus out of him, and he thought prayer was in order, so he said, "Dear St. Anne[9] help me." Then, thinking to give a little extra weight to his petition, he added, "If you help me, I will become a monk." Pretty quickly he discovered that he was O.K., but he was stuck with the promise he had made.[10] So on July 17, 1505, he was admitted as a novice to the Order of St. Augustine at their friary in Erfurt.

We know that Martin was a good monk because, after he no longer was one, he wrote, "I was a good monk." He fasted and prayed and mortified the flesh and tried to excel in austerity and asceticism. He willingly performed the most menial of monkish chores, including cleaning out the privy. He also studied like the dickens, and suffered from chronic constipation. He was often depressed and melancholy.[11] When in these lugubrious moods, he would see the devil and a gaggle of assistant devils waiting around to lure him into temptation. Some people scoff at such things, but we know that in Luther's case these were no vain imaginings, because we have it as a solidly attested fact that Luther once threw an inkwell at the devil. He also said he was tempted all the time by *"concupiscentia."*[12]

What Martin was doing was saving his own soul by the

[9] St. Anne is the patron saint and protector of miners. Luther wasn't a miner, but his father was, which made it all right for him to call on St. Anne.

[10] In later years, after he had ceased to be a monk, he explained his vow as *"terrore et agorre mortis subitae circumvallatus,"* which means, "I was scared as hell at the time."

[11] Excessive study combined with constipation tends to give one a gloomy outlook on life.

[12] This isn't what you think it is. It means "self-love" or "being too much turned in on oneself."

accepted method of the day. He worried all the time that though he kept all the monkish rules better than anyone else and was usually properly despairing over his sinfulness and resisted temptation like all get out, he would go to hell anyway. The only other thing for him to do was to confess his sins to his confessor and seek absolution, which he did almost every day. Sometimes he would confess for as long as six hours at a time, leaving insufficient hours to commit enough sins to make a decent confession the next day. Sometimes he had to rack his brain for anything and everything even faintly resembling a sin just to fill up the time. Naturally, his confessor, whose name was Johann von Staupitz, got awfully bored with all this. One day after Martin had confessed for five or six hours and left and then raced back into the confessional shouting, "I forgot a couple of things," Staupitz hit the ceiling and said, "Martin, if you must confess, please go out and commit some interesting sins like parricide or blasphemy. The least you could do would be to have a go at adultery, because I'm so fed up with all this junk you're spouting that I can't bear it for even one more session."[13]

Though they didn't seem to do him much good, there is no evidence that the young friar Martin Luther entertained even a faint uneasiness as to the spiritually salubrious effect of mortification, confession, penance, etc., until he was sent by his friary on a business trip to Rome. His excitement at the prospect of visiting the Eternal City was comparable to that of a country bumpkin who had never been farther than the county seat suddenly heading for the World's Fair. Rome, Martin knew, was where the religious action was. It would be a spiritual blast, and he was going to make the holy scene.

[13] It is not recorded if Luther took Staupitz's advice.

When he got there, though, it wasn't all that holy. His first jolt was when he went to confession, and the confessor didn't seem to give a hoot one way or the other about his sins. Also, the Italian priests didn't give a hoot about the mass, either, and could rattle off three or four complete masses by the time Martin got to the gospel. Then they would shout at Martin, *"Passa! Passa!,"* which is Italian for "get the lead out." He didn't think this was very pious of them.

He observed that some of the priests were deficient in faith.[14] He was unable to dodge the fact that the clergy in not-inconsiderable numbers frequented the red-light district, and that these sporty-type priests considered themselves highly moral so long as they confined their sexual activity to women. All this might have upset him only temporarily, but he went to climb the Scala Sancta.[15] When he started at the bottom he was sorry that his parents were still living, thus depriving him of the privilege of releasing their souls from

[14] Some, when they came to the part of the mass at which the bread and wine were supposed to be turned into the body and blood of Christ, would say, "Bread thou art, and bread thou wilt remain," and "Wine thou art, and wine thou wilt remain." They thought this marked them as men of liberated spirits and great humorists.

[15] The Sacred Stairs, or Pilate's Stairs. These are the steps Christ climbed to be sentenced by Pontius Pilate. They have been thoughtfully transported from Jerusalem to Rome and placed in a church convenient to pilgrims who climb them on their knees, pausing to kiss each tread and say a prayer. Pilgrims who reach the top receive all kinds of fine indulgences, and can release several souls from purgatory. They are privileged to name the souls they want released, making it possible to unchain a departed father or brother or former girlfriend while keeping their mothers-in-law safely stashed away for a few million more years.

purgatory. He decided to release the soul of Grandpa Heine instead. But by the time he got to the top his knees were pretty stiff, and he said, "There must be an easier way."[16] Although he went right on being a good Catholic for some time after this, historians concur that this incident was the first gleam of the Protestant Reformation in the eye of its father.

Not long after returning from Rome Martin moved from Erfurt to Wittenberg. This was a good move for him because many people called Wittenberg "The gem of Thuringia."[17] It happened that the Elector Frederick of Saxony, or Frederick the Wise[18] as he was known, had founded a university at Wittenberg and rather hoped to make it the intellectual center of Christendom. Things hadn't been working out that way, though, a situation which he blamed on the faculty. He felt the professors were a shabby lot, which is how trustees frequently feel about the faculty. Scouting around for new teachers, he asked the Augustinians to recommend a few, and they told him that Martin Luther at Erfurt was smarter and better read and more scholarly than almost anybody and should be a hot-shot as a university professor.[19] So Frederick hired him, and he held this job for the rest of his life. He had tenure.

[16] Some authorities claim that he also said, "I think this is a lot of malarkey."

[17] Others referred to it as "that stinking sand dune."

[18] Frederick was sort of like the governor of a state, or a junior-grade king. He was called "the Elector" because his position gave him a vote in electing the Holy Roman Emperor. He was called "the Wise" because he took forever to make up his mind.

[19] Martin had earned his Ph.D. by this time, only back then they called it the *licentia magistralis*. This sounds kind of dirty, but isn't.

In addition to being professor in the university,[20] Luther was also pastor of the Collegiate Church of All Saints. This church was famous for its growing collection of sacred relics. A 1509 catalogue lists 5005 relics in its possession, including a tooth from St. Jerome, four bones of St. Augustine, six of St. Bernard, four hairs from the Virgin Mary, three pieces of her cloak, and four from her girdle. Also, it had several relics of Christ, among them a wisp of straw from the stable at Bethlehem, one piece of the gold brought by the Magi, and one strand from Jesus' beard. The adoration of these holy souvenirs on All Saints' Day would give you enough indulgences to reduce a soul's stay in purgatory by 1443 years, either your own, or any other soul of your choice. By 1520 the collection had grown to 19,013 items, which, of course, raised considerably the collection's power over purgatory, as the adoration of 19,013 items can get you up to 1,902,202 years and 270 days off your sentence. It also raised considerably the tourist business in Wittenberg.

One would imagine that Martin Luther would have been delighted with the Roman Catholic system of indulgences, what with thousands of pilgrims flocking to his church to adore all those saintly relics, receive remission of sin, and paying hard cash for the privilege.[21] Surely the Elector Frederick was delighted. Remember, he was trying to make Wittenberg the intellectual center of Christendom, or at least of Germany.

[20] Luther came to the university as professor of moral philosophy, but soon traded that for the chair of biblical theology. It was hardly worth the effort, though, as he went on lecturing on whatever he wanted to talk about anyway.

[21] Maybe none of them paid very much, but when you are selling indulgences by the gross, it all adds up. In the indulgence business the turnover is what counts.

The merchants of Wittenberg were delighted. Presumably, the university was delighted because it received a big cut of the proceeds, and universities always need money. But Martin was not delighted. He preached three sermons in 1516 expressing his disenchantment with the system of indulgences. He reasoned that if the Pope is able to release souls from purgatory, then why doesn't he be a good sport and release them all right now? Besides, he said, true remission of sins depends upon true contrition on the part of the sinner, and who can know that except God?[22]

Nothing much happened as a result of these sermons except that Frederick the Wise was unenthusiastic about them. However, it was his opposition to the system of selling indulgences that finally landed Martin Luther in the soup, thus precipitating the Protestant Reformation.

A Hohenzollern named Albert of Brandenburg, who by ecclesiastical law was not old enough to be a bishop, was bishop of two sees (Halberstadt and Magdeburg) and wanted to be archbishop of Mainz.[23] This was going to cost a packet, Albert knew, and since he was short of ready cash he arranged to borrow from the banking house of Fuggers, instructing them to conduct negotiations with the Pope. This was Leo X, one of the Medicis, who liked carnivals, gambling, and hunting, not to mention several other things best not mentioned. He always wore long hunting boots, which were rather a nuisance when someone was supposed to kiss his toe. He didn't work

[22] All scholars agree that Luther's theology on this issue is not to be faulted, but that he betrays here a weak grasp of the intricacies of ecclesiastical finance.

[23] You probably think he wanted it for the honor of the thing, but Mainz was a very rich archdiocese, and it was the dough that Albert was after. Albert is a case of simple greed.

very hard and was always broke. He is not considered a great success as Popes go. After quite a bit of bargaining,[24] Albert got the job, and the Pope threw in the right to dispense indulgences in Albert's sees for a period of eight years. Leo was also to receive a cut of the indulgence money for the purpose of building St. Peter's—or at least that's what he said he was going to do with his share.

The best seller of indulgences around was a monk named John Tetzel. Tetzel was a huckster of extraordinary ability, a specialist in the hard sell. He printed material extolling the joys of purchasing indulgences, and sent it ahead of him so as to break down sales resistance. He always arrived in town accompanied by a brass band, preceded by a cross bearing the papal arms and the Pope's decree of indulgence[25] held high on a fancy pillow. The cross was planted in the marketplace, and Tetzel preached a sermon which went like this:

"Listen, you sinners and sons of sinners, God and St. Peter are calling to you. They are saying that you don't have a prayer of making it to paradise without some outside help, and I'm here to give it to you. And once you've taken care of your own sins, listen to the voices of your dear dead relatives. They are saying, 'You ingrates, think of all we did for you and now we lie here in flames, from which you could set us free and transport us to eternal bliss except that you are too cheap to cough up a quarter of a florin.' Remember, my dear Christian friends," Tetzel would conclude, "that this indulgence is

[24] Leo priced the archbishopric at twelve thousand ducats for the twelve apostles. Albert countered with an offer of seven thousand ducats for the Seven Deadly Sins. They finally compromised on ten thousand ducats, probably for the Ten Commandments.

[25] This decree was known as "the bull," but the Pope didn't see anything funny about it.

a real bargain, for it includes participation in the merits of the saints. This offer is for today only." Then, as a final come on, he said a little jingle:

> Sobald das Geld in Kasten Klingt
> Die Seele aus dem Fegefeuer springt

which means:

> As soon as the coin in the coffer rings,
> The soul from purgatory springs.[26]

Tetzel did not make his pitch in Wittenberg,[27] but he did get into the next county, and a goodly batch of Luther's parishioners, knowing a spiritual bargain when they saw one, went over and bought indulgences practically by the gross. Then they would go to Luther and ask him to honor them. Luther got mad and dashed off a protest against indulgences, and nailed it to the door of his church. This seems rather silly unless you remember that in those days the church door was sort of a community bulletin board, and people were always sticking things on it as a challenge to debate. Luther probably had to tear down a few other angry statements so as to make room for his. This challenge is known in history as the Ninety-five Theses.[28]

---

[26] For really tough customers Tetzel claimed that this indulgence he was hawking was strong enough to forgive a man "who had violated the mother of God."

[27] Frederick the Wise kept him out because he didn't want anyone cutting into the indulgence business at All Saints.

[28] Historians like to make a big thing out of Luther solemnly nailing the Ninety-five Theses to the church door. Probably about all that happened was that Luther banged his thumb and swore a little. It is generally acknowledged that Luther was a cusser of championship caliber.

Luther was surprised as all get-out when nobody wanted to debate his Ninety-five Theses because practically everybody said this was great stuff! The people didn't care much one way or the other about his theological arguments against indulgences. What they liked was the part where he called the Pope a greedy, grasping bastard.

Luther nailed the theses to the church door on the eve of All Saints' Day,[29] and things immediately went from bad to worse. The printer distributed many copies of the theses intended for professional theologians only, but they soon got around to the general public. Luther always claimed to be a modest, insignificant person who sought no fame or public acclaim for himself,[30] though there is some doubt about this, as he did nothing whatever to diminish his personal publicity. What he did was to write commentaries on his Ninety-five Theses, putting in stuff he wished he had included in the original, but he was so mad at the time that he forgot.

Naturally, Rome heard about the nasty things he was saying and would have cracked down on Luther right then except that Luther was off in the wilds of Germany and hard to get at. Also, Luther's popularity was growing, and Rome didn't

[29] October 31, 1517, to be exact. This is supposed to be one of the great dates in history, comparable to Marie Antoinette's pronouncement, "Let them eat cake," or the invention of bourbon whiskey. Unfortunately, we cannot be as precise about the dates of these occasions as we are about that of the Ninety-five Theses.

[30] He once wrote the archbishop referring to himself as "scum of the earth" and spoke of "my insignificance and untrustworthiness," but he went on to advise the archbishop (whom he called "your sublimity" and "your paternity") and to give him merry hell over the Tetzel affair.

want this local fuss to get out of hand.[31] So Luther was summoned to Rome to explain himself, but he was smart enough not to go.[32] He ended up agreeing to go to Augsburg, which wasn't nearly so far, and tried to explain himself to the cardinal.[33] The cardinal, however, had his mind on who was going to be the next Holy Roman Emperor since Maximilian was obviously on his last legs, so nothing much came of it.

To condense a lot of history which would only bore you, Luther spent the next three years debating and writing and shocking the pants off orthodox Catholics. He recommended, among other things, that saints' days be abolished, along with indulgences and pilgrimages to Rome. He also recommended that priests be allowed to marry because "many priests need a woman." He was against divorce,[34] but held that it was O.K. for a woman with an impotent husband to go to bed with another man provided that he wasn't married.

Obviously, Rome couldn't have a priest talking like this. Since priests in Rome who needed a woman either patronized a brothel or, if they could afford it, kept a mistress, the Curia couldn't see the problem. Somebody came up with the bright idea that if you couldn't bust Luther, why not buy him, so

[31] Not everyone in Germany was for Luther, though. There were two schools of philosophical thought in German universities at the time: the nominalists and the realists. The nominalists hated the realists, and the realists hated the nominalists, but the realists and the nominalists got together to hate Luther.

[32] He told the Pope his health was not good at the moment, and anyway he had been to Rome.

[33] His name was Thomas de Vio, cardinal of San Sisto, but he was called "Cajetan." Luther didn't think much of Cajetan, saying that he was no more fitted to handle the case than was an ass to play a harp.

[34] He said he thought bigamy was better, but he didn't say why.

Frederick the Wise was discreetly informed that if he could shut Luther up, the Pope would make Luther a cardinal and give Frederick the Holy Golden Rose. A holy golden rose doesn't sound like much of a gift to us, but Frederick thought it would be a great status symbol. This didn't work, although Frederick got his rose anyway.

Also, the Curia decided it might be good public relations for Tetzel to take the rap, so they framed him. They claimed he had two illegitimate children, and what was worse, he padded his expense account. Tetzel retired to a monastery or something and died of chagrin, although not before Luther had written him a comforting letter saying, "Don't take it too hard. You didn't start this racket."

Rome finally decided it would have to bust Luther after all, so it excommunicated him and told the Diet of Worms to make it stick.[35]

It was decided to butter Luther up a bit, so the Emperor, Charles V, wrote him a letter which started off, "To our noble, dear, and esteemed Martin Luther."[36] When the papal legate saw a copy of the letter he remarked, "Zounds! that's no way to address a heretic,"[37] but the Emperor offered Luther, in addition to honeyed words, a guarantee of safe conduct if he would show up at Worms and defend himself, which Luther

[35] A diet, in this case, doesn't have anything to do with food. It was a sort of national congress presided over by the Emperor. It is called the Diet of Worms because it was held, this time, in the city of Worms, and in no way refers to the character or personality of the members of the diet.

[36] Some authorities insist that it read, "To our dear, honored and pious Dr. Martin Luther," but you know how authorities are.

[37] The legate's name was Girolamo Aleandar. He spent a lot of time looking for a cure for syphilis.

did. The upshot of the matter was that when they asked him to recant he said that unless they showed him by scripture that he was wrong, which up to now they hadn't, he wouldn't. Then he added the words dear to the heart of every Stalwart Christian and the most famous phrase in Protestant history. In ringing, dramatic, courageous tones Luther shouted, "Here I stand! I cannot do otherwise. God help me. Amen."

Unfortunately, this isn't what he said, except for the "God help me. Amen" part. What he said was something along the lines of, "I can't do it because my conscience tells me not to, and it isn't a good idea to go against your conscience."

This didn't make much of an impression on Charles V, so he made a speech saying that he came from a long line of Christian Emperors, Kings, dukes, and the like who had upheld the Catholic faith through dying for it if need be, and that he was going to do the same.[38] Then he declared Luther a heretic and gave him twenty-one days to get home before the Diet proceeded against him.

So Luther threw a farewell party for all his friends and supporters at Worms,[39] and on April 26, 1521, headed out of town for Wittenberg. He didn't get to Wittenberg, though, because Frederick the Wise, who had a low opinion of the Emperor's promise of safe conduct, staged a kidnaping and hid Luther in Wartburg Castle for almost two years. During this time of exile Luther grew a beard and told people his name was "Junker George." He had a soft life at Wartburg, except that he suffered from constipation, piles, and insomnia.[40] He also discovered that the devil spent quite a bit of

[38] He died from eating too many eel pies.

[39] He served them Malmsey wine.

[40] He sent out for some laxatives in May, but they didn't get there until October.

time at Wartburg, and Luther was forever hearing him rattle
the sacks of hazelnuts lying about, or racing up and down the
steps with his cloven hoofs making an awful racket, or sneak-
ing into Luther's room in the form of a big black dog.[41] This
didn't help much to pass the time, so Luther decided to translate the New Testament into German, which he did.

When Luther finally got back to Wittenberg, for all practical
purposes the show was over because the Protestant Reformation had gotten up a full head of steam. There was an awful
lot of work to be done, of course, and Luther spent the rest
of his life doing it. All Reformations need principles on the
theory that if they don't have them, they are vulnerable to the
charge that they are unprincipled, so Luther got together
some principles, which were: (1) The priesthood of all be-
lievers, (2) The supreme authority of the scriptures,[42] (3)
The mass in the vernacular, and one other one that I forget,
but which I think had something to do with the ruler of a
country deciding whether it was a Protestant or a Catholic
country. He also fiddled around with the mass, and took some
altars out of the churches, and banned prostitution in Wittenberg.

Also, he got married.[43] Roman Catholic historians have a

[41] Luther once found the devil on his bed and had to throw
him out the window.

[42] The scholars refer to this principle as *sola scriptura* because it
sounds nice.

[43] He also liked drinking. He had a mug with three rings around
it—the top one, he said, for the Ten Commandments, the middle
for the Apostles' Creed, and the bottom for the Lord's Prayer. It
delighted him that he could drain it down to the "Amen" of the
Lord's Prayer, whereas his friend Agricola could hardly ever get
beyond the Eighth or Ninth Commandment.

habit of claiming that Luther started the Protestant Reformation because he wanted to get married, but they have a tendency to get Luther mixed up with Henry VIII, which isn't surprising as Martin and Henry looked a bit alike, both being on the paunchy side, and both of them popped off about anything and everything all the time, not to mention other habits they had in common. Anyway, we know that Henry was favorable to the Reformation because he wanted to get married, only he already had a wife and the Pope said he had to keep her. In Martin's case it may have been that he was sick of the celibate life and wanted to get married but couldn't because the Pope wouldn't let him as he was a priest, but this would be difficult to prove. The facts seem to be that all the priests who had joined the Reformation were doing it but Luther, and he finally decided, as Calvin did a little later, that one ought to marry just to spite the Pope and help do away with the celibacy of the clergy. His wife's name was Katherine Von Bora, a former nun who had joined the Reformation and was looking for a husband. Luther tried to help her and said he would fix it up for her to marry a Dr. Glatz. Katherine said no, she wasn't that hard up. She said Dr. Glatz was repulsive, and anyway, who wants to have a name like Mrs. Glatz. So Luther married her himself, and it worked out fine. They had six children, which is pretty good for a fellow who said he wasn't interested in sex, and besides he was forty-two when he started. He said a lot of profound things about marriage, such as, "Women were created with large hips so that they should stay at home and sit on them," and "Marriage is when you wake up in the morning and there is a pair of pigtails on the pillow which weren't there before."[44] He

[44] He also said that if your wife won't accommodate you, go see the maid, but he may have been misquoted.

appreciated the advantages of marriage such as Katie making the bed every day, whereas when he was single he had had to make it himself, once every year. After he got married he also found that he was frequently overdrawn at the bank, but then, he liked the way Katie talked to him because she addressed him as "My Dear Doctor."[45] Sometimes instead of "Katie" he would have a little fun and call her "Kette," which means "chain," but evidently she didn't mind.

Not that life was entirely a bowl of cherries for Martin after he got back from Wartburg and got married. He got himself involved in the Peasants' War of 1525,[46] and said some things about peasants, better not quoted in a family-type book, which peasants have held against him down to the present.

Then there was the difficult business of Philip of Hesse. It was important for Luther to keep the good will of Philip for reasons we won't go into here except that it had to do with the Schmalkaldic League. Philip was a Stalwart Reformed Christian who liked girls awfully well,[47] but didn't care much for his wife. As he was getting along in years, his conscience began to bother him, and anyway, he was slowing down quite a bit, and he felt he ought to confine himself to one girl whom he had thoughtfully selected after years of shopping around. Her name was Margaret van der Saale. What he wanted to do was to marry her without divorcing his wife, since as a Stal-

[45] You may think this a little odd, but it is better than what lots of women call their husbands.

[46] That was the one that got started when the Countess of Stulingen told her peasants to go pick some strawberries and gather some snails, and they didn't want to.

[47] He was sometimes called "That syphilitic Evangelical." If this seems a little harsh, we must keep in mind the fact that people were pretty censorious back then.

wart Christian he was opposed to divorce on principle. Luther said he would study and pray about it, to which Philip replied, "You do that." Luther finally found out that it is divine law that a man shall have only one wife, except under certain conditions which, by a rare coincidence, Philip of Hesse fulfilled. He said that it is O.K. for a man to double up on wives if his wife has leprosy, or if a man is a prince or a King. Philip said his wife didn't have leprosy but that he was sure as heck a prince. There was one catch to it, Luther said. A bigamous marriage had to be kept a secret. "Well, all right," Philip said, although he observed that since people wouldn't know he was married to Margaret, they would think he was still whoring around. Luther said that generally people would be more disposed to countenance whoring around than bigamy, so Philip had his own court chaplain perform the marriage in secret. But it got out anyway, and it didn't do Luther any good.[48]

Luther was getting pretty old by now, and complained all the time about the bad morals and coarse manners of the young people, and how the government didn't do a damn thing but collect taxes. He said he was going to retire, but never got around to it, and on February 17, 1546, while preaching a sermon at Eisleben, he had a heart attack and died.

John Calvin, the other great Reformation figure, was more pious and less earthy than Martin Luther, and confined himself to hanging and burning heretics for his kicks, whereas Luther was a bit more of a Stalwart Christian sport than Cal-

---

[48] Historians, unfortunately, don't tell us how much good it did Philip.

vin. Some people prefer Calvin's style, and others like Luther better. One thing you have to say in Luther's favor: He did start the Protestant Reformation—and you know how that turned out.

John Calvin

John Calvin's name was not John Calvin. It was Jean
Cauvin. He changed it to John Calvin for excellent reasons,
but he failed to tell us what they were. He was called "The
second patriarch of the Protestant Reformation,"[1] but he
started life as a Roman Catholic because when he was born
(July 10, 1509) the Protestant Reformation hadn't happened
yet.

You probably think that John Calvin was a Swiss because
he spent most of his adult life in Geneva. As a matter of fact,
he almost didn't go to Geneva at all. Where he really wanted
to go was Strasbourg because it was supposed to be a very
intellectual town, but he couldn't since there was a war going
on around there at the time, so he picked Germany as the
next best place. To get to Germany from where he was, which
was Italy, he had to go through Geneva. He said, "I had re-
solved to pass quickly through this place without stopping
more than one night in the town." But he hardly ever got out
of Geneva after that, except for about three years when they
kicked him out.

John Calvin was born at Noyon, which is in Picardy, which
is in France. His father was a fairly prosperous lawyer with
excellent connections at the local R.C. church. Through these
connections, he was able to secure for Jean, or John, several
lucrative benefices. This meant that John was appointed to

---

[1] He was also called a number of other things best not recorded
here.

several priestly posts with handsome salaries attached. The fact that he was a child and not qualified for the jobs was no handicap because there were plenty of unemployed priests around who could be hired to perform John's duties for a mere pittance, and John could keep the difference.[2] John never did become a priest. The Church shaved his head, though, as a sign that he was free-loading off it. With money in his pocket, John was able to enter the University of Paris at the age of fourteen. There he learned Latin, the errors of Humanism, dialectics, and studied the writings of Augustine of Hippo and the theses of Duns Scotus. He also became proficient in nominalist terminism.[3]

All this time John Calvin was a devout and pious Roman Catholic. His father had intended him for the priesthood, but he soon perceived that his son was too smart to be a clergyman, and switched him to law because, as Theodore Beza, Calvin's biographer, noted, John's father saw that law was where the real dough was.[4] Also, the old man lost his connections with the Roman Catholic Church at Noyon about this time, although John was able to hang onto his benefices and avoid working for a living. He graduated from law school, but instead of setting up in business, he went back to Paris to study humanistic culture and write a commentary on Seneca's *Treatise on Clemency*. Since there was very little demand for humanistic culture or commentaries on Seneca, he turned to other things, including conversion to Protestantism.

As a result of his conversion, he had to leave Paris, so he

[2] You have to remember that this was the bad old days when there were politics in the Church.

[3] Nominalist terminists are not highly thought of today, but it was the thing to be back then.

[4] This isn't exactly how Beza put it, but this is what he meant.

went back to Noyon and resigned his benefices and was put in the pokey "for an uproar made in the church." When they let him out he left town[5] and wandered around for a while. It was during this time that he spent a night in Geneva and was persuaded by William Farel, the leading pastor of the city, to stick around and help set up the Protestant Reformation there. Calvin said he didn't want to because he wanted to be a scholar instead of a crusader, but Farel said, "I denounce unto you, in the name of Almighty God, that if, under the pretext of prosecuting your studies, you refuse to labor with us in this work of the Lord, the Lord will curse you." This did the trick.

Calvin, whose idea of a proper Christian city was a place where everyone thought correct thoughts and behaved themselves, saw that making Geneva into a "city of God" wasn't going to be any snap. The people had rather carefree ways. In the Madeleine quarter every third house was a tavern, and the red-light district was doing a land-office business.[6] Debauchery was very popular, and the parties the Genevese were forever throwing were said to be a caution.

To help the citizens think correct thoughts, Calvin drew up a confession of faith which everyone was to accept.[7] To help them behave themselves, he drew up rules of conduct. These rules included prohibition of playing cards on Sunday; spending time in taverns; cursing and swearing; trying to commit suicide; possessing a copy of *The Golden Legend;* saying *requiescat in pace* over a husband's grave; betrothing one's

[5] He could take a hint.

[6] It had been necessary to establish a special police guard to keep the clergy from patronizing it.

[7] Those who didn't were graciously permitted to get out of town.

daughter to a Catholic; having your fortune told by a gypsy; eating fish on Good Friday; giving a priest a haircut; saying there is no devil or hell; arranging a marriage between a woman of seventy and a man of twenty-five; saying the Pope is a good man; criticizing the doctrine of election; expressing a distaste for the practice of executing people for holding heretical religious views; and singing songs uncomplimentary to John Calvin.[8] There was also a rule that everyone had to go to church and "listen to the sermon devoutly." Three men were put in prison one Sunday because they laughed during the sermon. Another was "severely reprimanded" because he criticized the sermon and said he liked the former preacher better.

One would suppose that the Genevese would have appreciated these reforms, as all this was for their own good, but not all of them did. A pastor named Caroli, who was very strong on the doctrine of the Holy Trinity, said he was afraid Calvin might be holding heretical views on the subject and suggested, or rather insisted, that Calvin affirm in public in front of everybody that he believed every item in the Apostles', Nicene and Athanasian Creeds down to the last Very God of Very God and all that. This upset the people some because you can't have a leader who is shaky on the doctrine of the Holy Trinity. It upset Calvin some, too, because he was so mad he got sick for a while. When he got over being mad and sick, he attacked the problem with his customary administrative skill and kicked Caroli out of the ministry, which tidied up the whole mess.

The real trouble, though, arose over certain practices in the Church. The city council decreed that Christmas, Easter, As-

[8] There were more of these rules, but this will give you the idea.

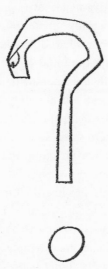

cension, and Pentecost should be celebrated as religious festivals; that the baptismal font should be at the front door of the church; and that unleavened bread should be used in the communion service. In fact, the council said the ministers had to use unleavened bread or they couldn't preach their sermon. Calvin, who knew that God intended that leavened bread be used in the communion service, said he wouldn't obey,[9] so the council sent him packing.

Calvin went to Strasbourg, where he had intended to go in the first place, and improved the time by introducing the custom of congregational singing[10] and extempore prayer. Extempore prayer means that instead of using a prayer book the preacher makes up the prayers as he prays them. Extempore

[9] Theologians have a way of knowing what is vital.

[10] He didn't permit pipe organs, though. At Geneva he melted down the lead pipes of the organ in his church and made them into cups for communion wine.

prayers have many advantages over prayer book prayers, as anyone can see, especially preachers. For one thing, the preacher can pray about what is on his mind at the moment instead of what was on the mind of the author of the prayer book when he wrote it. For another thing, the preacher praying extemporaneously can aim the prayer at a situation that is troubling the parish or at people in the congregation whose behavior isn't quite up to snuff, so in effect an extemporaneous prayer gives the preacher an opportunity to preach an extra sermon. Also, extempore prayer has benefits from God's point of view, inasmuch as He has heard all the prayer book prayers a good many times and is probably bored with them and maybe doesn't listen very closely to them any more, but He more or less has to listen to extempore prayers because He might learn something He didn't know before. Congregations, as a rule, are somewhat less enthusiastic about extempore prayers than preachers are because, while they are old stuff, prayer book prayers are short, whereas extempore prayers usually run on for quite a while.

Calvin also got married during his stay in Strasbourg. He wasn't much interested in sex, but he was interested in finding a woman who would look after him, and as servants were hard to get and undependable and also rather expensive, he decided that the sensible and economic thing to do was to find a wife. Since Calvin loved drawing up rules and drew them up for practically everything, he drew up a set of rules by which to judge the candidates for the title of Mrs. Calvin. He even wrote them down for the edification of posterity. Anyone who aspired to be Mrs. Calvin, he wrote, must be chaste, agreeable, modest, frugal, patient, and be "solicitous for my personal health and prosperity." Modern girls might not think that Calvin was prime husband material, but apparently husbands were not easily come by then or maybe the girls weren't so fussy and a number of candidates made themselves available. He was engaged once, and the wedding date set, but Calvin heard rumors that she was an undesirable character (she was addicted to the wearing of jewelry and the eating of snails) and broke the engagement. He eventually married a widow named Idelette de Bure, of whom he became quite fond. He grieved deeply when she died, and regretted very much that he had to keep an appointment the evening she was dying.[11]

After he had been in exile for two years the City Council of Geneva decided things were worse without Calvin than with him, and invited him back to take up where he had left off. This tickled Calvin, but he didn't answer the letter for six months. Then he "reluctantly" accepted the offer. He said he still preferred being a scholar. After his recall, Calvin set about organizing the city so that it would be a place where the word of God would be the absolute authority in matters of faith, morals, and daily conduct.[12] Calvin said he would tell them what the word of God was on the subjects of faith, morals, and daily conduct.

He organized the pastors into what he called "the Venerable Company." It was the duty of the Venerable Company to meet once a week to discuss the Scriptures, and once a month to point out each other's shortcomings.[13] He organized a body of twelve laymen known as "the Elders" or "the Consistory."

[11] He had a committee meeting to attend.

[12] What else is there?

[13] The Venerable Company would have preferred meeting once a month to discuss the Scriptures, and once a week to point out each other's shortcomings. It isn't easy to point out all those shortcomings when you have a crack at it only once a month.

It was the duty of the Elders to point out everybody's short-comings.[14] They also were charged to "admonish affection-ately" those who were seen to err in their thinking or conduct.[15]

To promote right conduct, Calvin closed all the taverns in Geneva and opened up a chain of drinking places (he called them "abbayes") run by people of whom he approved. He said he wasn't making a nickel out of the deal, which maybe he wasn't because he never showed much interest in money. But it did give him an opportunity to draw up some more rules, and he thought drawing up rules was more fun than spending money, anyway. Each tavern was to display the Bible in a prominent place, and the patrons were to engage in religious conversation. Everyone was supposed to say grace both before and after their drink.[16] No one could play cards for more than an hour at a time, and the joints were closed at nine o'clock. They were not a commercial success. Calvin also helped the citizens in the perplexing problem of selecting godly sounding names for their children. This thoughtful as-sistance came about because a man presented his son to be baptized with the name Claude. The minister said he pre-ferred the name Abraham. The father said he preferred Claude. Calvin was asked to settle it, so he drew up some more rules. The names Angel, Baptist, Evangelist, Sunday, Sepulcher, Easter, Pentecost, and Jesus were forbidden, as were Tyvet, Monet, and Claude. The father who started the whole thing finally settled for Ami, which, as anyone can tell, is much more godly than Claude.

[14] Except the Venerable Company's, of course.

[15] They were sometimes so affectionate in their admonitions that the admonished ended up dead.

[16] For serious drinkers this involved quite a bit of praying.

Calvin always claimed that he was a compassionate and kindly man, and that there was a simple explanation of the fact that in one four-year period fifty-eight citizens of Geneva were executed, a record up to that time.[17] He said it wasn't because he was severe, but because under his administration the snoopers were more efficient and the laws were applied impartially. Not everyone agreed with his explanation, but then, all great men have their detractors. Calvin was usually sad when he had to have people executed, but he did publicly rejoice when one Jacques Gruet was beheaded for blasphemy, because Gruet's offense was to tack a placard to Calvin's pulpit reading, "When you irritate us too much, we explode." What Stalwart Christian would disagree that the punishment was just and well-deserved? Historians agree that Gruet's execution was the act which made Calvin's power secure in Geneva as this convinced the Genevese that he meant business, although some say his prohibition of the wearing of slashed breeches helped.[18]

With Gruet and slashed breeches disposed of, Calvin was able to get on with the building of the City of God with little opposition. Stalwart Christians tend to be either Stalwart Defenders and Builders of the Faith (building institutions, sniffing out heresies, cultivating princes and Kings—things like that) or Stalwart Thinkers of the Faith (sitting around manu-

[17] Most of them were knocked off for the crimes of treason, witchcraft, and heresy, and all right-thinking people assumed that they had it coming. Calvin, of course, defined treason, witchcraft, and heresy.

[18] Slashed breeches were considered very stylish in Geneva, but Calvin thought they contributed to spiritual pride and the love of luxury. Also, he couldn't find anything in the scriptures which permitted the wearing of slashed breeches.

facturing theological propositions, dreaming up doctrines, constructing philosophies). John Calvin was both a Stalwart Christian Defender and a Stalwart Christian Thinker. As a defender he ran Geneva, preached 286 times a year, saw scores of people every day, carried on a voluminous correspondence, attended the interminable meetings of the council and the Consistory, and visited the sick, plus spending much time trying to help the Protestants of France who were being subjected to the thought control and persecutions of the Catholic Inquisition, because Calvin thought it was outrageous that French Protestants were persecuted for their religious beliefs.

As a Stalwart Christian thinker Calvin ground out a prodigious stack of writing. His writings fill fifty-nine quarto volumes. He felt that in order for the people to know what was proper for them to believe he would have to write it down, which he did in *The Institutes of the Christian Religion,* a work much admired by theologians and Presbyterians today.[19]

Calvin was at his very best when writing on such subjects as a defense of the stoning of false prophets. His prose style reaches lyrical heights in a passage which reads:

"We ought to trample under foot every affection of nature when it is a question of (God's) honor. The father should not spare the son, the brother the brother, nor the husband his own wife. If he has some friend who is as dear to him as his own life, let him put him to death."

Some deluded and theologically befuddled people said Calvin was harsh and ruthless in his treatment of heretics, but he was always able to adduce ample justification from the Scriptures, especially from the Old Testament (he always did

[19] They don't read it much, just admire it.

like the Old Testament better than the New), for stamping on those who, he thought, dishonored God.

Most literate people, given an association test, would respond to the word "Calvin" with "predestination," though they might experience difficulty in rendering a lucid explanation of what predestination is. John Calvin did not invent the doctrine of predestination. Augustine and Luther beat him to it. But all authorities hold that he developed it to its highest and purest form. A life of John Calvin without an explanation of the doctrine of predestination would be like *Playboy* magazine without the centerfold, so the author, who, of course, has a scholar's grasp of the subject, will attempt to render a condensed account of it for the lay mind.

To understand predestination, it is necessary to begin by assuming the correctness of Calvin's basic premise.[20] Calvin's basic premise was that the sovereignty of God is the number one fact of the universe. In practice, this means that God is awfully important, and that men are more or less negligible.

The number two fact of the universe is that Adam was a sinner, and since all men are children of Adam, they have all inherited his sinfulness. The number three fact is that there is a heaven and a hell, both supposedly inhabited.

But since everyone is a sinner, who is in heaven? The average, run-of-the-mill theologian of Calvin's day was likely to answer, "Why, those people who, by their good and upright life or their correct connection with the one true Church, have earned the right to be in heaven are there."[21] Calvin disposed

[20] It is necessary to make this assumption about any other theological proposition also.

[21] Theologians differ widely on what it takes to earn a spot in paradise, but a theologian generally believes that whatever it takes, he's got it.

of this manifest nonsense by replying that since God is everything and man is nothing, who goes to heaven and who goes to hell is a decision handled by God alone. God could, in all justice,[22] send everyone to hell, because aren't we all sinners?

But, said Calvin, God is also merciful, and he sent Jesus Christ who, through his work as prophet, priest, and king, mediates God's saving grace to mankind.

In that case, some critics said, then heaven is full and hell empty.

Not at all, Calvin replied. God only elects or predestines some people to be saved by divine grace. There are plenty left to populate hell to the glory of God.

On what basis does God sort out the elect from the damned, the critics asked. You aren't supposed to ask that question because it demeans the majesty of God, as any fool can plainly see, Calvin replied.

Does this mean that even little babies who perish in their cribs are predestined to hell, they asked. Of course, Calvin said—some of them, anyway. When someone would complain that this hardly seemed fair of God, Calvin would patiently explain that they had it backward—God didn't do a thing because it was a good thing to do, as most dunces and boneheads thought. God did what God did, and because He did it, it was a good thing to do. This is known as the inscrutable wisdom of God. Calvin was enthusiastic about the inscrutable

---

[22] Calvin was strong on the justice of God. God is always perfectly just, he said. When critics answered that this justice is hard to see in some situations, Calvin replied that God is also obscure, and when His ways seem unjust to us, He is at the moment only being obscure.

wisdom of God, as it clears up many difficult theological questions.

How do I know if I am one of the elect, predestined for paradise, people would ask. You'll know, Calvin would say. If I am elected for salvation, is it not possible that I might get unelected, others would ask. Does God change His mind? Calvin would answer.

Perhaps the most concise way to summarize the doctrine of predestination is this: If you are good, God gets the credit. If you are bad, you get the blame. Therefore, if God sorts you into the pile consigned to hell, you deserved it. If He decides to send you to heaven, you don't deserve it; you're just lucky. This is known as "divine grace." People who know they are elected find great comfort in the doctrine of predestination. Those who don't know if they are elected or not are less enthusiastic about it.[23]

The last nine years of Calvin's life in Geneva were not too eventful. There wasn't much opposition left to bother him, as by this time the opposition was mostly banished, in jail, or dead. So he just plugged along, building the City of God and persecuting an occasional heretic. One man was punished for sleeping in church and awakening with a great noise, but he was let off lightly when he said that the noise he made was because his legs hurt and was in no way intended as a commentary on the sermon. There was a little excitement when Calvin's brother's wife was apprehended in the act of adultery with Calvin's hunchback servant, Pierre Daguet. In her defense, we have to remember that opportunities for fun and games were scarce in Geneva, and she couldn't be too choosy. A little later Calvin's stepdaughter Judith was caught doing

---

[23] Calvin knew he was elected.

the same thing.[24] Calvin was a little depressed over all this,[25] so to take his mind off it he went out and built the University of Geneva.

Calvin had been a frail child, and he was a sickly man.[26] He suffered, at various times, from bad circulation, ulcers, hemorrhoids, gout, rheumatism, kidney stones, fever spasms, difficulty in breathing, trembling of the fingers, migraine headaches, insomnia, bloody sputum, and other ailments too numerous to mention. In the spring of 1564 most of these diseases were afflicting him at once, and he knew that he had had it. So he got busy drawing up a set of rules, mostly a final set of doctrines which right thinkers were to believe, and some directions for running the Church after his departure. He also made a will which is said to be praiseworthy for the sobriety with which it enters into detail. It would be. His last instructions to the Church were "to make no changes nor innovations . . . because all changes are dangerous and . . . harmful." Most churches have made valiant efforts to follow this counsel ever since. On May 27, 1564, he gave up the ghost.[27]

The one large blot on Calvin's otherwise speckless life as a Stalwart Christian is his controversy with a Spanish physician named Michael Servetus. Dr. Servetus was, evidently, a scientist of parts, but he was more interested in theology than in medicine.[28] He published a book titled *De Trinitatis*

[24] With a different fellow.

[25] Some of the less pious citizens thought it was a great joke that couldn't have happened to a nicer guy.

[26] "Sickly" refers only to his physical health, of course.

[27] At about eight o'clock in the evening, European Standard Time.

[28] He discovered the pulmonary circulation of the blood seventy

Erroribus, which was about as bad as it sounds. In it, he called the doctrine of the Trinity "a sort of three-headed Cerberus," and Stalwart Christians, obviously, couldn't put up with such talk. Things got too hot for him in Spain, so he moved to Vienne,[29] France, and changed his name to Villeneuve. He didn't, however, change his ways. He went right on attacking such prized orthodoxies of Stalwart Christendom as the Nicene Creed and the efficacy of infant baptism. He also rejected predestination, the pre-existence of Jesus, and the verbal inspiration of the Scriptures. While writing a manuscript exposing the errors of Stalwart Christendom, he made the mistake of sending a draft of it to Calvin. Calvin kept it,[30] and Servetus had to rewrite the whole thing. Calvin sent Servetus a copy of *The Institutes of the Christian Religion,* of which he had plenty lying around the house, and Servetus marked it up with his own commentaries on Calvin's ideas[31] and sent it back to Calvin. When Calvin read Servetus' marginal notes on his (Calvin's) book, he said that if Servetus ever showed up in Geneva he would never leave it alive if he,

---

years or so before William Harvey came up with the idea. No one would ever have known that Servetus made the discovery except that he included it in a sort of footnote in one of his theological pamphlets called *Christianismi Restitutio.* Since doctors are not, on the whole, avid readers of theological tracts, Harvey got the credit for the discovery by announcing it in medical journals.

[29] Vienne is also famous as the location of Pyramide, held by gourmets to be the world's finest restaurant. Unfortunately, it wasn't there during Servetus' time.

[30] Calvin gave the mealy mouthed excuse that he had lent it to a friend who had neglected to return it, but Calvin was able to produce it as evidence against Servetus at a trial eight years later.

[31] The commentaries were somewhat critical in nature.

John Calvin, could help it.[32] Calvin managed to call the attention of the French Inquisition to Servetus' doctrinal laxity. Calvin and the Inquisition did not think highly of each other, as we have seen, but hunting heretics makes strange bedfellows. The Inquisition then clapped Servetus in jail and condemned him to death by slow fire. When some people said that it wasn't nice of Calvin to deliver Servetus to the Inquisition, Calvin said he didn't do it.[33]

Servetus managed to escape from jail, but he had a problem of where to escape to. He was under sentence of death in Spain[34] as well as in France. Italy looked like the best bet. The catch was that the only convenient way to get to Italy was through Geneva. Unfortunately, he had to go through Geneva on a Sunday, and since everyone in Geneva had to go to church on Sunday, he went. He was apprehended while listening to Calvin preach.[35]

At the trial the authorities did what authorities often do: they tried to frame him. They charged him with being an immoral person, but the manufactured evidence wouldn't hold up. So they had to rest their case on his denial of the Trinity, infant baptism, and predestination. They also nailed him for saying that Moses was wrong about Palestine being a land flowing with milk and honey, that he held views similar to those of the Anabaptists, and that he was "trying to bring

[32] Authors, as a class, tend to be sensitive to literary criticism of their works, but this seems a bit excessive.

[33] He lied about it is what he did. But since he lied to the glory of God he thought it was O.K.

[34] The Spanish Inquisition had hired Servetus' own brother to find him and bring him back. They intended to burn him over a fast fire.

[35] At least he didn't have to sit through the whole sermon.

back in vogue the chimerical fantasies that were originally invented by the Gnostics." Servetus was denied a lawyer,[36] and on October 26, 1553, he was condemned to be burned alive, which was done the next day. Calvin, to his credit, pleaded for mercy for Servetus. Instead of burning him, Calvin said, maybe they just ought to hang the bastard.

Nevertheless, the good people of Geneva have had a slightly uneasy conscience about their handling of Servetus' case. A few years ago they erected a memorial to him[37] on the spot where he was burned alive. The inscription, roughly translated, says: "We, the people of Geneva, erect this memorial to Dr. Michael Servetus, just in case there are those who feel that John Calvin was a trifle severe in his treatment of Servetus. But," the inscription concludes, "we want to affirm that we are good Calvinists."

Also to their credit, the good citizens of Geneva have taken further measures to ensure that the name of Servetus shall not die. They named the local football team after him.

[36] The authorities said he could lie as well without one.
[37] A little old rock behind the hospital is what it is.

Heloïse and Abelard

Almost everybody has heard of Heloïse and Abelard, but they haven't heard very much. For most of us the two names conjure up images of star-crossed lovers, romantic frustrations, noble self-renunciations, and other delightful things which thrill us through and through as long as they are happening to someone else, but which aren't a great deal of fun when they happen to us.

Unfortunately, the facts in the case of Heloïse and Abelard don't entirely support our vague impressions of innocent young love and tender sighings in moonlit gardens. What we have here is more like a lengthy episode in *Peyton Place* with gobs of suffering and blood and raw sex, not to mention large helpings of unbridled ambition, cupidity, vengeance, and other horrendous facets of human nature on which American housewives gorge themselves every afternoon via the soap operas. So delicate readers who want to preserve their illusions are warned off at this point. Read no farther. Sturdier types may continue.

First, let us look at Abelard. Peter Abelard was born in Brittany in 1079 at Palais or Le Pallet, which is the same place, but it goes, or went, by either name. His father's name, we think, was Berengarius. We know his mother's name was Lucia, because Abelard once wrote of her *"Carissima mihi mater mea Lucia,"* which translated sounds more like something a boy ought to say about his mother than it does in Latin.

When the kids were grown, Berengarious and Lucia broke up housekeeping and entered the religious life—he in a monastery and she in a convent—which indicates that they didn't find each other irresistible. Abelard, as the eldest son, would have inherited the estate (which was fairly substantial), but he wanted to be a famous scholar more than anything, so he relinquished his inheritance to a younger brother and took off to improve his mind. It was apparent even at this early stage of his career that he was afflicted with what was then called *acuta ingenia*. This isn't a disease, although some people claim it is, but means simply "a keen intellect."

Abelard first studied under the celebrated Nominalist philosopher Roscelin, but he thought Roscelin was awfully dumb, an attitude which he didn't keep secret, so this class was soon out. Next, he had a crack at the Realists, studying under William of Champeaux at Notre Dame in Paris, but William was just as dumb as Roscelin, and Abelard would get up in class every day and debate William and show him up for an idiot, which annoyed William quite a bit and also the other students so somehow they got the message across to him that they would just as soon as he didn't come around any more.

Abelard then decided it was silly to keep going to school when you already knew more than the teachers, so at the age of twenty-three he set up in the school business himself and was such a success that he ended up as head of the school at Notre Dame which he had left in disgust a few years before. When he acceded to the post at Notre Dame, he modestly stated that he was the only philosopher in the world worthy of the name. He also stated that, up to this time, he had led a life of chastity, which we have no reason to doubt, though Paris has never been the easiest of places to lead a life of chastity, and one wonders why Abelard felt it necessary to assure us on this point. Also, by this time he had taken up with theology and had become a tonsured cleric in minor orders, which of course goes quite well with chastity.

At any rate, whether he had or whether he hadn't led a life of chastity is rather unimportant because pretty soon after this he didn't. The reason he didn't was Heloïse, who was about sixteen in the year 1116, which was the year Abelard first set eyes on her. He was much taken with her, though he was, from her perspective, an ancient thirty-seven-year-old, and exclaimed, *"Cum per faciem non esset infima, per abundantiam literarum erat suprema."*[1]

We don't know a great deal about Heloïse's antecedents, but from what we do know it is probably just as well. A sixteenth-century historian named Popire Masson insists that she was the illegitimate child of a priest named John, but how would he know? Others claim that her Uncle Fulbert, her guardian with whom she was living when Abelard met her, was in fact her father. Uncle Fulbert was also a priest, an important canon of Notre Dame Cathedral, so if he had fathered Heloïse, he shouldn't have.

To our horror we discover that Abelard immediately set out to seduce Heloïse. We know this because Abelard tells us that this is what he did. He mentions that since he was rich, famous, and handsome, as well as brilliant, charming, and learned, it was highly unlikely any woman could resist him.

[1] This means, "She is some babe, and smart, too." Abelard also said that her learning had made her known throughout France, a judgment we would be inclined to doubt inasmuch as Abelard wasn't entirely objective about Heloïse, except that Peter the Venerable, abbot of Cluny, said about the same thing, and it is hard to doubt Peter the Venerable. Anyway, we do know that Heloïse could read and write.

Being a theologian, Abelard had a thorough grasp of the doctrine of original sin, which he employed cleverly to set up the seduction. He had noticed that Uncle Fulbert, priest though he was, was susceptible to greed and pride even though they are two of the Seven Deadly Sins and supposedly ruin a man's chances for heaven. Abelard told Fulbert that the heavy demands upon him as the most popular teacher in the world left him no time to find an apartment, let alone look after it, so he would be willing to move in with Fulbert—as a free boarder, of course—but would in exchange endeavor to impart some of his priceless knowledge to Heloïse. We can see that this was an unlikely story, since how can a man who hasn't time to find an apartment have time to teach a kid of sixteen? But Uncle Fulbert was so tickled at the prospect of a cheap education for his niece that he failed to see through Abelard's flimsy proposition and told him to move right in.

Abelard no sooner unpacked his bags than he got down to the serious business of seduction. We don't know exactly how many class sessions took place before Abelard started making passes at Heloïse, but it couldn't have been many as he had hardly sent out his first laundry before he began writing love poems about Heloïse and setting them to music, so we can be certain that he had something to sing about. He wrote stuff like

> Suscipe, Flos, florem
> quia flos designat amorem;
> Illo de flore
> Nimio sum captus amore,

which brings tears to our eyes in the original, and really grabs us when we learn that it means "you are best compared to a flower, so I am giving you a flower to let you in on the fact that I have a hankering for you." Abelard practically flooded Paris with these musical love poems, anonymously, of course, since a man in Holy Orders is supposed to be thinking about Nominalism and the three major points of his next sermon and things like that instead of carnal experiences, and people in the streets were humming them and saying the lyrics to one another. Abelard discovered that seducing girls and writing love poems, let alone composing music for the poems, took a lot of time and energy, so he quit working on new lectures and did what professors usually do after the cares of life and the pleasures of the world take the bloom off their academic idealism: He began pulling out his old lectures and giving them over. This caused no little bit of derogatory comment from his students. One would have thought that Uncle Fulbert would have heard the talk and noticed the sappy expression which Abelard no doubt wore continually and put two and two together, but evidently he didn't. What did happen was that Uncle Fulbert surprised Abelard and Heloïse in what is euphemistically referred to as an embarrassing position, and since this wasn't part of the curriculum he had in mind for Heloïse, he gave Abelard the heave-ho.

Shortly after this Abelard received a letter from Heloïse in which she said she was writing *"cum summa exultatione,"* which means she was happy as all get-out, because she was pregnant. We do not know if this news made Abelard as happy as all get-out or not, but he did contrive to swipe Heloïse from Uncle Fulbert's house and take her to Brittany to his sister's. He was able to manage this trip, his biographers say, because their love affair was at its hottest at Passiontide, which seems appropriate, although as Stalwart Catholic Christians they should have been observing Lent with prayer and self-denial but evidently weren't, and it was Easter Vacation at Abelard's school so no one noticed his absence.

When Uncle Fulbert discovered that he was to be a great-uncle, he blew a gasket. He was so apoplectic that Abelard says you would have had to see the old boy throwing a fit to have believed it. Abelard did the manly thing, though, and offered to make an honest woman of Heloïse on the condition that the marriage be kept secret as it would do Aberlard's reputation no good if it were known, and after all, the world's greatest philosopher does have to think of his reputation. Fulbert agreed, and Abelard trotted off to Brittany to tell Heloïse he had graciously decided to marry her.

Much to his surprise, Heloïse said no. She had several noble reasons for her attitude, such as that Cicero and St. Jerome and other unimpeachable authorities had held that philosophers hadn't ought to get married, but what these arguments added up to was that Heloïse didn't think Abelard was husband material. She also said she didn't mind being his mistress but that she preferred not to be Mrs. Abelard, an attitude we find strange in a Stalwart Christian, but perhaps she knew something we don't know.

Abelard, however, insisted, and since Heloïse was not very good at refusing him anything, they parked the baby (a boy named Astralabe) with Abelard's sister and went back to Paris to get married.

They thought they could keep the marriage a secret, but you know how people talk, so Abelard put Heloïse in a convent, which he thought would quiet things down, but it didn't. Uncle Fulbert was still a little irritated with Abelard even though he had married Heloïse. So Fulbert, just to show he hadn't gotten over being peeved, rounded up some cronies and went to Abelard's rooms, and, as Abelard related the incident, "they deprived me of that part of my body with which I had committed the deeds of which they complained." We tend to think that this was somewhat unkind of Uncle Fulbert, but then, he may have wanted to help Abelard achieve the goal of a celibate philosopher-scholar, which in those days was considered about the best thing you could be, and since Abelard hadn't been a notable success at celibacy[2] up to then, perhaps we should take the attitude that this was all for Abelard's own good.

From this point on the story is pretty much downhill. Abelard decided to re-evaluate his vocational options and, finding himself extremely well qualified for the life of a monk, entered a Benedictine Abbey. Heloïse took vows as a nun, not because she wanted to, which she didn't at all, but because Abelard told her to, and she was in the habit of doing what he told her to do. He didn't say exactly why he told her to, but it is hinted that he wanted to protect her morals, which, if this was his reason, is certainly admirable.

Anyway, both Heloïse and Abelard lived on for quite a while and spent most of their time writing letters to each other, which are still available to you in any convenient library, only it would probably just depress you to read them. Abelard's letters, for example, tell us a lot more than we care to know about life in a monastery, although we suppose Heloïse appreciated all this trivia. He also wrote some poetry, in one of which he mentions that Heloïse keeps complaining that if

[2] Abelard was accused of spending vast sums on prostitutes, which he may or may not have done, as we have no evidence in the way of canceled checks made out to ladies of the evening or sales receipts for medicine to cure the pox. But if he had, then Uncle Fulbert's informal surgery certainly saved Abelard a lot of money.

her salvation depends on her forgetting what fun sex was when she was still carrying on with Abelard, she is for damn sure headed for hell, which seems rather tactless of her, considering Abelard's condition.

Abelard died in 1142, at the age of sixty-two. Heloïse lived on for another twenty-two years, which would have made her sixty-four when she gave up the ghost. They are buried together in a cemetery at Père-Lachaise. It is said that when Heloïse's body was brought to lie beside Abelard, Abelard reached out his arms to her, which you probably think is only a legend, but is really no more incredible than the rest of the story.

Thomas de Torquemada

Though he began his career as a Stalwart Christian at about the age of fourteen when he entered the Order of St. Dominic, no one suspected that Thomas de Torquemada was a stalwarter Christian than almost anybody until he was fifty-eight years old. In fact, his life up to that time was so run-of-the-mill ordinary Christian no one thought it worthwhile to write down anything about him, so we don't have any records to depend on for this period. We do know that his father, Pero Fernandez de Torquemada, was a rather insignificant member of the Spanish nobility, and that his uncle, Juan de Torquemada, was cardinal of San Sisto,[1] which doesn't make him as important as it sounds because in fifteenth-century Spain you could hardly walk down the street of any fair-sized town without bumping into several cardinals.

We also know that Thomas was a brilliant student, taking a doctor's degree at an early age. He majored in philosophy and theology, which was a great help to him later when he had to figure out sound philosophical and theological rules for persecuting heretics, but this didn't seem to help him much in his early career as a Stalwart Christian. What did help was

[1] He was the one who wrote deep and learned works on the dogma of the Immaculate Conception, but he probably got to be a cardinal because he was Spain's No. 1 champion of the doctrine of papal infallibility, a dogma which Popes find even more appealing than the dogma of the Immaculate Conception, important as that is.

some small local reputation for extraordinary austerity of life,[2] which caused the authorities to promote him to prior of the monastery of Santa Cruz of Segovia. Not many of us would want to be prior of the monastery of Santa Cruz of Segovia, but Thomas thought it was a pretty good thing for a thirty-two-year-old Stalwart Christian. The monks under his supervision didn't like him much because he set an example of piety and self-denial considerably more rigorous than they cared to follow, but there wasn't anything they could do about it. After all, it isn't good form for you to be having a thick steak when the boss orders a soy-bean cutlet. Also, his sister didn't like him much because when he inherited the family fortune, he refused to provide her with a dowry but put her in a convent run by the Dominicans because he said he knew what was best for her.[3]

To understand how Torquemada got to be the stalwartest of Stalwart Christians, you need to know a little bit about the political situation in Spain at the time, a rather uninteresting subject to be sure but necessary to our biography. Spain wasn't exactly a country then. The most important part of Spain was Castile, of which Isabella was Queen. Her husband, Ferdinand, was King of Aragon, not in a class with Castile as a country, which annoyed Ferdinand considerably.[4] In the north there was the nothing kingdom of Navarre, although the French and the kingdom of Aragon fought over it whenever they got up the energy and had nothing better to fight

[2] He wore a hair shirt and never ate meat.

[3] Since Thomas was a Dominican he got her in the convent at wholesale prices. He used the money he saved on some of his building enterprises.

[4] In Castile he was only the Queen's consort, which doesn't do much for the ego of a King.

over at the moment. That left the kingdom of Granada in the south, very rich and prosperous and controlled by the Moors, who were Mohammedans and, as infidels, a stench in the nostrils of all Stalwart Christians.

Now you understand the political situation in fifteenth-century Spain except for the Jewish problem, which isn't as easy to understand. There were 250 Jewish communities in Spain at the time, and they had gotten along exceedingly well with their Stalwart Christian neighbors until about the middle of the fourteenth century when people began to notice how prosperous they were. Under Pedro the Cruel, who wasn't very nice even as Kings go, Stalwart Christian mobs murdered, burned, pillaged, and in other ways knocked the Jews around for a while. But the Christians finally got bored with all this, since murder and pillage is exhausting work, and decided to convert the Jews instead. So they sent out missionaries under the leadership of Friar Vincent Ferrer, who later got a sainthood for his efforts, and told the Jews that they should become Christians because the Christian God was a God of love, and besides if they didn't, the Christians might kick them around some more. One or the other of these arguments must have gotten to the Jews because this was one of the most successful evangelistic campaigns in all Christian history.

Unfortunately, the Stalwart Christians didn't think about the fact that once a Jew was baptized, all the professions and trades from which Jews were barred by law would now be open to him. The Jews didn't forget, though, and almost before you could say *In Hoc Signo Vinces* the baptized Jews were the leaders in the professions of medicine, law, teaching, politics, and almost any other that could be made into a good thing. One of the main reasons for this was that the

Spanish nobility had a marked distaste for work, whereas the Jews didn't mind working at all. After a while the Spanish nobility was, on the whole, pretty broke, and rather than go to work it started the custom of marrying rich Jewish girls.[5] The upshot of all this was that Spain was full of baptized Jews,[6] and a Spanish nobility possessed of *Limpieza* or "blood purity" was almost as rare as a Communist at a meeting of the John Birch Society.[7]

Naturally the Spanish Stalwart Christians hated the converted Jews. They said they hated them because the *marranos* weren't really Christians, just pretend Christians, who went to mass and confession but secretly ate Jewish food and things like that, which was a distinct threat to the true faith. Actually, they probably hated them for the same reason that normal, healthy-minded, envious, no-account people hate the successful and the rich today, especially if the successful and the rich have done a lot for them as the Jews did for the economy of Spain and the sagging fortunes of its nobility. People like to think they are hating other people for sound religious reasons, though, so the Spaniards said that you had to remember that the Jews were Christ-killers, so no matter what bad things you did to them, it was pleasing to the Christian God of love who was so superior to the wrathful and vindictive Jehovah Jew-God.

There isn't much else you need to know about conditions

[5] This superseded the inflexible Stalwart Christian custom of marrying only Stalwart Christian girls. However, Stalwart Christians tend to be more broadminded when they are dead broke.

[6] They were called *conversos* when you wanted to be polite, or *marranos*, which means "accursed" or "swine," when you didn't.

[7] Spaniards considered *Limpieza* the greatest status symbol there is—next to money, of course.

in mid-fifteenth-century Spain except maybe that it was the
strongest Christian region in Europe with priests, nuns, monks,
bishops, and cardinals everywhere and everybody went to
church all the time and to confession and all that. The top
clergy spent their time at politics or soldiering,[8] leaving the
lesser clergy to do all the religious work such as preaching
and hearing confessions. The lesser clergy relieved the tedium
of their jobs by seducing women in the confessional booths,
which must have been rather uncomfortable. Nobody seemed
to mind this very much, but when the archbishop of Santiago
tried to rape a young bride for whom he had just performed
the marriage ceremony, the people got sort of sore and kicked
him out for a while. And, of course, since Spain was full to
the brim and sloshing over with faith, the Pope kept sticking
his nose into the politics of the Spanish countries, and especially devising new ways to get some of that good Christian
money to Rome, though the Stalwart Christian Kings and
Queens and dukes weren't terribly enthusiastic about this.

Now to get back to Thomas de Torquemada. As we have
noted, he was a competent but not overly distinguished cleric
for the first six decades of his life, and should have been
thinking about taking his social security and retiring, but he
wasn't. What he was thinking about was the Jews. Torquemada was kinky about Jews. Whereas average Stalwart Christians only hated Jews a few hours per day, Torquemada hated
them practically full time.[9] He hadn't been able to do much

---

[8] The archbishop of Toledo loved to play soldier and was always
dashing around in a scarlet gown with a big white cross on it, leading his private army in the most attractive war he could find at the
time.

[9] Sometimes, just for a little variety, he hated the Moors, but he
didn't have much spare time left over from hating Jews.

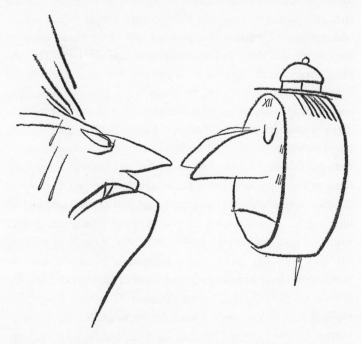

about it up till now, but when his chance came, he managed to take advantage of it.

Torquemada had known Queen Isabella since she had been a little girl, and after she became Queen this paid off when she appointed him her official confessor. Being confessor to the Queen is a very nice job with short hours and good pay and whatnot, but it wasn't what Thomas had in mind. So he began pestering Isabella to institute the Inquisition in Spain and let him run it. He also pestered Ferdinand.

Isabella was a pious Christian, but she was more interested in creating a united Spain than she was in hunting heretics. Ferdinand was a Christian, though not overly pious, and wanted to start a war with Granada but didn't have the ready cash. So Torquemada showed Isabella that to have a pure and united Spain you had to do something about the Jews, and he showed Ferdinand that if you could burn a lot of Jews for heresy, the Crown could confiscate their property, and Ferdinand would then have enough money to wage a high-style war with dandy uniforms and flashy weapons and good horses. These were convincing arguments, so after some fussing around with the Pope, who thought he had the right to run Inquisitions and get a cut of the profits, Thomas de Torquemada became head of the Inquisition in Castile and Aragon in October of 1483.

Ignorant people usually believe that Torquemada invented the Inquisition, but he didn't. We shouldn't hold this against him, though, because he probably would have invented it if Pope Innocent III hadn't already thought it up back in 1200 or thereabout. We can't, of course, give Innocent III all the credit, either, because the church had been persecuting heretics a good long time before 1200. Since the Roman Catholic version of the Christian faith was put together something like an Erector Set, you couldn't remove one pillar of Catholic truth without all the other Catholic truths tumbling into a heap, and then you would have to go to all the trouble of putting it up again. Every now and then, of course, some idiot would open his big mouth and say some true doctrine was false, and all the bishops and theologians would quiver with anxiety because if you could convince some people that a true doctrine is false, which you usually can, then it would be no trick at all to convince people that a false doctrine is true, and once people start believing that one false doctrine is true, they will in all likelihood jump to the conclusion that all true doctrines are false, and then things would be in an unholy mess.

The logical solution to this problem is to keep anybody from saying anything about Roman Catholic truth except that it is true, but this isn't as easy as it sounds. Prior to Innocent III[10] the diocesan bishops would have a go at heresy hunting when it was absolutely necessary, but their efforts were amateurish and not very effective.

When a particularly pesky bunch of heretics known as the Albigenses[11] started raising Ned in the south of France, Innocent decided to do something about it, and he invented the Holy Office, which is the proper name for the Inquisition and sounds much better. Instead of letting the diocesan bishops hunt heretics on a hit-or-miss basis, the Holy Office was placed in charge of the Dominicans, who were in a position to give it full-time attention, standard operating procedures, and refine the methods of torturing recalcitrant heretics.

Many wrongheaded critics of the Inquisition have accused it of delighting in torturing heretics, but this is terribly unfair. When the Holy Office opened up for business in a city, it would begin with a procession to the cathedral and then a sermon by the highest-octane preacher available extolling the joys, blessings, and benefits of confessing your heresy right off, and the downright bliss obtainable by snitching to the author-

[10] Innocent III's real name was Lothario Conti, and history considers him a whiz as a Pope. He was a top-drawer thinker who pointed out that as Vicar of Christ on earth he had supreme authority in matters of faith and morals, but personally he was more interested in politics and tried to unite Europe in a kind of United States with himself as the boss. When people said he shouldn't because he had authority only in faith and morals, he replied that politics was a matter of morals, which, of course, cleared that up.

[11] In case you have forgotten, the Albigenses were a branch of the Cathari heresy. They preached Manichean doctrines and other repulsive ideas.

ities on your husband, wife, mother, father, siblings, aunts, uncles, and cousins you suspected of thoughts deviating from Roman Catholic truth. If you couldn't think of any relative to turn in, a longtime friend or business associate would do as well. Then any heretics had about a month to give themselves up voluntarily.

For stubborn types who had to be hauled in, treatment was still rather gentle. He would find himself in the cell with another prisoner who intimated that he, too, was a heretic, but was in fact a member of the Inquisition.[12] The cell was bugged, of course (there was a court stenographer listening in the next cell and taking it all down), and many a heretic was bagged this way, making it possible to burn him immediately without the unpleasant and time-consuming necessity of torturing him.

The real proof of the essential gentleness of the Holy Office, though, was its generosity in promising "grace" to an accused in return for a full confession plus the betrayal of a few friends. Most heretics thought it a good idea to confess and betray a few friends in return for a complete pardon, which is what they understood the word "grace" to mean. The inquisitor then would be forced to explain to them that there was a problem of semantics involved here, and that while grace could mean full pardon, it could also mean a state of being reconciled to God before you were burned at the stake, which was the meaning that the Inquisition attached to it. In defense of the Holy Office, though, it should be noted that many times it did partially remit penalties to heretics who confessed. A man named Vramo, who had ratted on a few friends

[12] This fake took care not to say outright that he was a heretic because this would have been a lie, and lying is a venial or sometimes even a mortal sin.

under promise of grace, saw his friends have their hands cut off and then drawn and quartered before being burned, whereas they just burned him whole.

For suspected heretics who failed to fall for these gentle suasions the Holy Office regretfully employed torture. It was pretty good at torture, having had plenty of practice. Actually, the torture was carried out by the secular authorities, as it wouldn't have been in good taste for an ordained clergyman to engage in that sort of thing, but there was nothing against an experienced inquisitor passing along a few tips on torture to the actual torturers. Some favored the rack, others the toasting of the feet over a slow fire. Most popular, though, was the water torture, which doesn't sound very bad but is. It is difficult to express a preference for one of these tortures over another, as all of them were rather effective.

With himself in charge of the Holy Office in Spain and an almost unlimited supply of healthy young monks to act as bloodhounds in searching out heretics,[13] Torquemada took out after the Jews like sixty.[14] In a few years he managed to burn at the stake between two and three thousand Jews, plus

[13] One young Dominican friar in Seville spent every Saturday clambering over rooftops in the ghetto sniffing the chimneys. If a chimney wasn't smoking, he took it as proof that this house was observing Jewish sabbath and ran them in. If you were a Stalwart Christian *marrano* and just having cold cuts that day, that was your tough luck.

[14] He had one of his monks write a guide for detecting a Jewish-pretend-Christian called *Censura et Confutatio Libri Talmud*. In the Preface, the author referred to Torquemada as "*Reverendissime pater noster, serenissorum regum confessor, Sancta Crucis Segobrinsis friar, generalis hereticorum inquisitor, quem Dominus Jesus dilexit*"—all of which we could translate for you, but it would be too fatiguing.

putting at least one hundred thousand in prison, which would have satisfied most people and given them a real sense of accomplishment.

But not Torquemada. He wasn't going to settle for being just a middling successful Stalwart Christian, so he got a law passed which expelled all Jews from Spain forever.

Torquemada didn't always get his way, of course.[15] Once when a town of Moorish infidels was captured, he recommended to the King and Queen that every man, woman, and child in the place should be put to the sword, but Ferdinand, who was more interested in money than in killing infidels, said he was horrified at Torquemada's recommendation, because all these people could be sold into slavery and the Crown could make a bundle, which is what Ferdinand did.[16] So that Torquemada wouldn't feel too badly about it, though, they permitted him to burn a few of the less salable citizens. A Stalwart Christian historian of the time reported that these "fêtes and illuminations [burnings] were most gratifying to the Catholic piety of our sovereigns."

The year 1492 is important in human history because that is the year Thomas de Torquemada retired. He was seventy-two years old, and a little run-down,[17] and anyway there isn't much for a professional Jew persecutor to do in a country that has run all the Jews out. So he went to the monastery at

[15] Who does?

[16] At first the Holy Office had been very profitable to the Crown, but by this time Parkinson's Law had set in, and the Inquisition had so many people on the payroll it had to hustle to find rich heretics just to pay expenses.

[17] He had gout, which is somewhat rare in a man who has spent his whole life on a diet.

Avila which he had been building for several years[18] and spent his time building more buildings onto it, as architecture was the second great love of his life, although by no means as great as his first great love. He lived until 1498, and these last years were peaceful and more or less undisturbed, except that he became almost paranoid about being poisoned because some other inquisitors had been murdered by heretical Jews who failed to understand that everything the Holy Office was doing was for their own good. Torquemada would never eat a meal without the horn of a unicorn and/or a scorpion's tongue beside his plate, as these are very effective in detecting and counteracting poison. This ran up household expenses considerably because, though scorpion's tongues are abundant, unicorn's horns are hard to come by and hideously expensive. Since he was never poisoned, we are led to the conclusion that unicorn's horns do work. On September 16, 1498, he received the last sacraments and pegged out from natural causes.

One of his biographers says that he was "the light of Spain, the savior of his country, and an honor to his order." Another tells us that he was "a pleasant, kindly, industrious, able and modest man, whose chief ambition in life was to imitate Jesus Christ."

We suspect that, on the whole, Thomas de Torquemada was satisfied with his life. He was never canonized, of course, but one can't have everything.[19]

[18] It was named the Monastery of St. Thomas. It would be.

[19] Sainthood was not withheld because of any soft-minded squeamishness on the part of Rome, because one of his fellow inquisitors was canonized. Torquemada didn't make it for the very sound reason that no miracles were ever reported at his tomb.

If he had any regret, it was probably that he did not possess *Limpieza* or the blood purity which he so highly prized. But there wasn't anything he could do about it because one of his grandmothers was a full-blooded Jew.

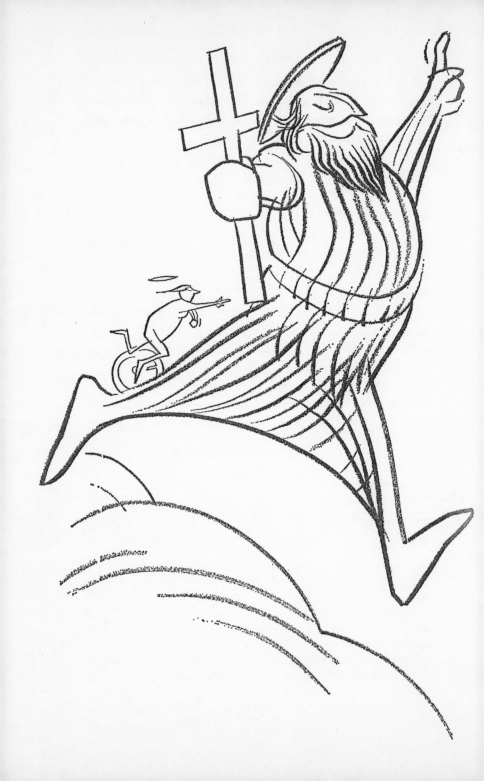

King Henry VIII

King Henry VIII of England, who was born June 28, 1491, got off to an early start as a Stalwart Christian. Since he had an older brother, it was not anticipated that he would ever be King, and what to do with leftover sons was something of a problem for royalty and the landed gentry back then because the oldest boy in the family, by law, inherited the whole package—Crown, family estate, etc. This was very nice if you happened to be the oldest son, but the family had to scrounge around to find something for the other kids, and it wasn't always easy.

One favorite device was to have the younger boys go into the Church. This wasn't as bad as it sounds because a prince could be pretty sure that Daddy would wangle him a bishopric before long, and though the clergy was supposed to be celibate, nobody really expected that all the clergy would be, especially princes and other nobility, and the Pope didn't say anything so long as they didn't marry the girl.[1]

Henry was marked for the clergy at a tender age, so he was educated in theology and stuff like that as well as trained to fill high clerical office such as bishop.[2]

[1] Some of the Popes were in no position to say anything, as they had their own establishments furnished with the lady of their choice.

[2] This training probably consisted of the sixteenth-century equivalent of double-entry bookkeeping and how to exact tithes from reluctant parishioners, as in those unenlightened days theology was considered to be a peripheral concern of bishops.

But theology was to play a large role in Henry's career, as we shall see. It began playing a large role rather early because Henry's brother, Arthur, who was supposed to be King as soon as Henry VII was gathered to his eternal reward, fouled things up by conking out at the age of fifteen, shortly after he had married Katherine of Aragon. Since this marriage had been good politics for England as well as having brought a fine price in dowry payments from the King of Spain, Henry VII didn't want all this to slip through his fingers and decided that he would marry his daughter-in-law himself inasmuch as he was a widower and could use a wife, especially a rich one. But Queen Isabella, Katherine's mother, said King Henry was a dirty old man and ordered him to send Katherine home, along with the dowry. The King couldn't let that happen, so he said how about if she marries my son Henry, which evidently was O.K. with Isabella because Henry, who was twelve at the time, suddenly found himself engaged to his sister-in-law.

So far as we know Henry didn't mind, but the Archbishop of Canterbury kicked up a ruckus because, he said, the law of Moses plainly states that a man shall not take his brother's wife as this is an unclean thing to do and God will see to it that such a couple shall be childless, which would be simply awful in the case of a King, as why else does a King bother to get married except to produce a male heir? Everybody agreed that it would be terrible to go against the law of Moses until some other theologian pointed out that Deuteronomy says that a man is supposed to marry his dead brother's wife and "raise seed," and then everybody agreed that Deuteronomy is a better guide in such matters than Leviticus, so the betrothal took place, only the Pope's dispensation, which was necessary to make it legal, didn't get there until after the celebration.

Henry VII didn't last long after this, and young Henry soon found himself King Henry VIII and the husband of Katherine. He seemed to like her pretty well, although he couldn't speak Spanish and she couldn't speak English.[3]

As a King, Henry was enthusiastic about religion. He was one of the most Stalwart Catholic Christians there ever was, going to mass three times a day and whooping off to war if the Pope needed defending, and things like that. He read one of Martin Luther's books and was so incensed by the heresy he found in it that he sat down and wrote a book exposing Luther for the scoundrel he was.[4] When a copy was presented to Pope Leo, who fancied himself an expert literary critic, the Pope admired the binding and said he was astonished that a busy King could have turned out a book, but he didn't say that it was good. However, he issued a bull which conferred on Henry the right to call himself Defender of the Faith, which tickled Henry because he loved titles and thought this one especially high grade as titles go.

Pope Leo hardly had time to read Henry's book as he died about three months after admiring its binding. Cardinal Wolsey, Henry's right-hand man, had long felt himself eminently qualified to be Pope, and Henry thought it would be nice to have an old buddy sitting in Peter's Chair, so he sent an envoy to the Vatican to cajole the cardinals into selecting Wolsey. But what Henry didn't know, although he should have,

[3] He gave her a missal and wrote on the flyleaf, in French, "I am yours forever," which he probably meant at the time, but which we now know was somewhat of an exaggeration.

[4] It took him two years to write it, but we must remember that he had other things to do.

was that a mere royal envoy was a babe in the woods among experienced Vatican politicians who had been playing the game for well over a thousand years. The envoy wrote to Henry that "there cannot be so much hatred and so many devils in hell as among these cardinals," which disillusions us a little as to the holiness of the Holy City, but we have to tell it like it is, or rather was, since we feel confident that conditions at the Vatican have improved vastly in the meantime.

The upshot of the election was that a Dutchman won the papal sweepstakes, which may or may not have been connected with the fact that he had once been the tutor of Charles V, the Holy Roman Emperor. So Wolsey had to go home still a cardinal, and Henry, probably to solace him, let him start a small war.[5]

To solace himself Henry had two mistresses, one a blonde and one a brunette, a logical selection if one is going to have two mistresses. The blonde's name was Elizabeth Blount, and the brunette was known as Mistress Carey, not because she was the King's mistress, which would have been too much even in the sixteenth century, but because her first name was Mary, and Mistress Carey sounds better than Mary Carey. Mistress Carey's maiden name was Boleyn, but she wasn't the one you have heard about. That was her younger sister Anne, who comes into the story pretty soon now. We mustn't be censorious of Henry for having a couple of mistresses because the mores were different back then, and biographers assure us that compared to other kings of the time, Henry was eco-

[5] Wolsey had no sooner returned to England than he beat up on a diplomat who said something he didn't like. If this seems unbecoming in a prince of the Church, we mustn't forget that a fellow doesn't lose out on being Pope every day, and Wolsey was pretty disappointed.

nomical in the matter of mistresses and would have had to have had several more of them than he had before endangering his status as a Stalwart Christian and Defender of the Faith.[6]

Henry had other worries besides keeping a blonde and a brunette happy. The Dutchman who beat out Cardinal Wolsey died. This was a cause of great rejoicing in Rome as he was among the most unpopular Popes ever, not an easy thing to achieve as there have been some spectacularly unpopular Popes in the history of the papacy. His unpopularity stemmed largely from his unfortunate tendency to tell the truth,[7] a personal foible looked on with suspicion at the Vatican. It was said in Rome that having the grace to die after a short papacy was his most popular act as Pope. The Romans erected a statue to celebrate the occasion.[8]

Anyway, Cardinal Wolsey told Henry that he would rather continue in the King's service than be ten Popes, but that it was now obvious that God's will had been short-circuited when the cardinals had failed to elect him before, and so maybe Henry had better get cracking and help fulfill God's will by politicking for Wolsey this time. One way or another, they persuaded Emperor Charles to write a letter to the Vatican backing Wolsey, but the Emperor—who had another candidate in mind—thoughtfully refrained from mailing the

[6] Unfortunately, these biographers do not tell us the maximum number of mistresses a King can have and still be considered a Defender of the Faith, but we infer that it is a lot more than two.

[7] He said the Vatican was a stinking mess of corruption, dirty politics, clerics of dubious character, and other un-Christian things, which it was, but people thought it was bad form for him to say it.

[8] It was a statue of the Pope's doctor.

letter until he received the news that his own candidate had it in the bag, so God's will was short-circuited again.

Another one of Henry's worries was the Queen's failure to produce a male heir. Also, he had begun to notice Anne Boleyn, a toothsome morsel according to historians although she had a strawberry mark on her neck and a malformation of her left hand. Our best information indicates that Henry proposed to discard Mistress Carey, Anne's older sister, as it would have been un-Christian to have had sisters for mistresses even if three mistresses didn't exceed the quota for Defenders of the Faith, and substitute Anne. But Anne thought it would be more Christian for Henry to discard his wife and make Anne Queen, which was a great deal more of a nuisance as wives are not so easily discarded as mistresses, or weren't in those days.[9]

Anne's attitude helped Henry to see that Leviticus had been right after all, and that he was actually living in sin with Queen Katherine, something no Christian King could put up with, so he took steps to annul the marriage. He told Katherine that his conscience would no longer permit him to keep her on as Queen, and even if his conscience would permit it, as a theologian of some standing he could plainly see that Holy Writ forbade him to do so.[10] Katherine reacted by weeping copious tears, and Henry did what any sensitive, kind-hearted husband would have done—he got the hell out in a hurry, muttering something like "all shall be done for the best."[11]

[9] Anne had undoubtedly noticed that being a King's mistress— while it had its advantages—offered very poor job security.

[10] The fact that it took him eighteen years to reach this conclusion should not be held against him, as theologians are notoriously slow to make up their minds.

[11] He failed to specify for whom it would be best.

He also told her it would be better if she didn't mention the subject of their conversation, but somebody mentioned it because pretty soon it was the gossip of London.

Only the Pope, whose name was Clement, could legally dissolve the marriage. This should have been easy enough because though the Roman Catholic Church has always stood for the sanctity of marriage and sternly forbids divorce, and if you were a blue-collar Catholic and wanted to get rid of the old lady you didn't have a prayer of getting the job done, the Church—in its wisdom and compassion—has always understood that Kings and the nobility and the monied upper classes have unusual burdens to bear and that it is a clear Christian duty to lift some of these burdens, especially an inconvenient wife. But, unfortunately, from Henry's point of view, King Charles of Spain, though he was also the Holy Roman Emperor, had recently sacked Rome and taken the Pope captive, although what a Holy Roman Emperor would want with a Pope named Clement is hard to figure out, and it was unlikely that Clement as the prisoner of Queen Katherine's nephew would be inclined to see things Henry's way.

When the Pope was finally free, Cardinal Wolsey sent a delegation of two bishops to present Henry's case. The Pope said he had heard by the grapevine that Henry wanted an annulment so he could marry a lady of doubtful virtue. The bishops replied that nothing could be farther from the truth, that it was Henry's sensitive conscience which would not permit him to live in sin that was the reason they were there. Was it not logical, they argued, that a King who needs a male heir to preserve the stability of the realm and also assure the continued prosperity of the Church in his land, would be looking around for a new wife once he had regretfully concluded that the old one had to go? They wanted the Pope to know,

they said, that Anne Boleyn was worthy of high praise as a
lady of maidenly modesty, sober, humble, wise, and noted for
her "constant virginity," as they put it. They were only kidding,
of course, especially about her virginity, as she had once been
banished from the Court for too much fun and games with a
chap named Lord Percy, but the bishops felt it unnecessary to
mention this to the Pope.

The Pope griped a lot about Henry's request. The Emperor
was still breathing down his neck, he said, and probably
wouldn't appreciate having his aunt's marriage annulled. Why
in hell didn't Henry have two wives, he asked the bishops.
After all, the papacy had granted Henry IV of Castile permission to marry a second wife, so there was good Christian
precedent for such a solution. Why couldn't Katherine discreetly retire to a nunnery, as she was a very religious type
anyway, and Henry could marry Anne Boleyn without the
necessity or inconvenience of an annulment? The bishops replied that this thought had occurred to Henry, but that
Katherine had proved uncooperative. The Pope then used
some swear words and said he wished Katherine were in her
grave, which would clear the matter up nicely. He finally
granted permission for Cardinal Wolsey to decide the case,
along with Cardinal Campeggio, an Italian, so that the pro-
ceedings would be impartial, because the fact that Cardinal
Campeggio was a buddy of Henry's and Henry had made him
bishop of Salisbury, which was quite a financial plum for an
impoverished Italian cleric, would in no way influence
Campeggio's decision. The Pope also promised to abide by
whatever decision the two cardinals reached, which was most
gracious of him as well as getting him off the hook.

The case was opened on the last day of May 1529. Henry
testified that he wasn't going to endure a bad conscience any

longer, so the Court had better get at it and dissolve the marriage.

Then the Queen testified that though she had been married to Henry's brother Arthur for a few months, she was "a true maid" when she married Henry, as Arthur was only fifteen and didn't know what it was all about. The Earl of Shrewsbury and the Duke of Norfolk then said that her contention was ridiculous, because they could testify from personal experience that fifteen-year-old English boys all knew what it was all about. Then John Fischer, bishop of Rochester, horned in and told the Court he had written a book on the subject proving that Henry's marriage could not be dissolved, a copy of which he just happened to have on him at the moment and which he would be glad to lend the Court for its edification.[12] The upshot of the matter was that Cardinal Campeggio courageously rendered the Court's decision which was that Court was adjourned for the summer.

It could be said that by adjourning the Court without a verdict that Cardinal Campeggio assured England's future as a Protestant nation, because Henry fired Wolsey as Prime Minister and declared himself the "Supreme Head of the Church and Clergy of England," a title formerly held by the Pope, and nobody wanted to argue with him about it. As Supreme Head of the Church, he no longer had to consult with the Pope about the appointment of English bishops,[13] so when the archbishopric of Canterbury conveniently fell vacant he appointed Thomas Cranmer who, by coincidence, had written a book proving that Leviticus was right and that

[12] Authors will do almost anything to publicize their books.

[13] He no longer had to pay Peter's pence to the Vatican, either, which was the traditional fee for the consecration of bishops, and wasn't as cheap as it sounds.

Henry wasn't really married to Katherine. The King felt he ought to marry Anne Boleyn pretty quick as she had given up her continual virginity and he had her pregnant, and he wanted his son to be legitimate and a proper heir to the throne, which is how any Stalwart Christian King would have felt about it since it was the only decent thing to do. So the new Archbishop of Canterbury expedited the matter, and Henry and Anne were married in plenty of time before their daughter was born. The Spanish ambassador thought so little of the event that he reported to his government that the King's concubine had born him a bastard daughter who had been named Elizabeth.[14]

Anne did ultimately produce a son, but he was stillborn, and pretty soon Henry's sensitive conscience began to bother him again because, as a theologian, he thought maybe the fact that Anne's sister had once been his mistress made his marriage to Anne illegal. Since he was getting pretty tired of Anne anyway, he investigated the matter carefully and discovered that, sure enough, this marriage was illegal, and besides he had taken a fancy to Jane Seymour. But Henry didn't think he could go through all that annulment business again, even though he was now Head of the Church in England and could be relied upon to render himself a fair and just verdict, so he had her head chopped off, which was much simpler in every way.[15] Ten days later he married Jane Seymour, who in due time presented him with a son and died twelve days

[14] A lot of people called her the same thing after she became Queen Elizabeth I, but for different reasons.

[15] He said she had been flirting with another guy whose name was Sir Henry Norris. In order to make his point the King chopped off Norris's head, too.

after giving birth, which in the light of Henry's marital record was probably the smart thing for her to have done.

Next, Henry married Anne of Cleves because her father, the Duke of Cleves, was a nuisance to the Emperor and Henry thought it would be nice to irritate the Emperor, and besides he had seen her portrait by Holbein and she looked awfully good to him. When she came over for the marriage, he discovered that Holbein had done a little improving on the original and also she was kind of stupid. So his Stalwart Christian conscience got to bothering him again and he was afraid that they weren't legally married in the eyes of God because she had once been engaged to someone else. He was, he told her, going to put aside the marriage, which action he was certain would be approved by the Church because he was the Head of the Church. Anne thought it was her turn for the chopping block and fainted dead away, but Henry revived her and said he intended to adopt her as a sister and set her up in her own establishment, which tickled her because she hadn't cared much for Henry as a husband but thought that as a brother he would be tolerable.

Next, he married Katherine Howard and made no secret of the fact that he judged her to be the best wife he had ever had.[16] He liked to pat her a lot, even in public, which she didn't seem to mind. The reason she didn't mind was probably because she had, as it soon came out, much experience in being patted. This might have been O.K., but after her marriage she went on letting other guys pat her, and eventually Henry found out, so off to the chopping block she went. Henry wasn't as robust as he had been and he hadn't been as

[16] Considering his matrimonial experience, this was no mean compliment.

lucky in love as he might have been, but he thought he was up to at least one more wife, who was Katherine Parr, twice a widow, so not without experience herself, and she outlived him, which certainly distinguishes her among Henry's wives.

Whatever his deficiencies as a husband, Henry had impressive credentials as a Stalwart Christian. He was a Stalwart Roman Catholic Christian to begin with, and a Stalwart Protestant Christian at the end. After he became a Protestant, there were no more cowled monks hanging around London, and the monasteries were dissolved, but by and large things went on about the same as before. The Lutherans had expected to prosper under Henry after he sort of joined the Reformation, but Henry hated the Lutherans, so they didn't. Henry was thoroughly orthodox, and upheld the doctrine of transubstantiation over against the Lutheran doctrine of consubstantiation. These two doctrines of the Lord's Supper or mass have important differences, although it is difficult to recall what they are. Henry held to the traditional liturgy of the Church, and he insisted on the celibacy of the clergy because he didn't want his priests contaminating themselves with sex.

His only real problem was the doctrine of the supreme authority of the Pope. He had to have something in place of that, and felt that he himself was qualified for the job but that maybe he needed a little help, so he copped Luther's doctrine of the supreme authority of the Scriptures and referred to the Bible as "that most precious jewel, the Word of God." This was wise of him because he could always find something in the Bible which backed up what he wanted to do anyway, and if the Bible is the supreme authority, who is going to make an issue of it?

There are those who are a trifle critical of Henry as a

Stalwart Christian, saying that his excessive boozing, wenching, gluttony, execution of wives and enemies, and one or two other small imperfections in his character are not entirely consistent with the best in Christian conduct. But he did make a good death as his last act on earth was to clasp the hand of Archbishop Cranmer, and anyway aren't we all flawed vessels?

King James I and the Stalwart Christian Committee

For centuries good Christians of stalwart Protestant persuasion have believed that God Almighty dictated the holy Scriptures word-for-word in Elizabethan English, the only authentic record of which is contained in the Authorized or, as it is popularly known, the King James Version of the Bible. Recent research, however, has established that this is not the case. King James VI of Scotland, or King James I of England as he was known after he succeeded Elizabeth on the English throne, not God, was responsible.

It may be arguable, and indeed has been argued, that it was God who was responsible for the Authorized Version, but that He accomplished His purposes through King James. Opponents of this view have pointed out that if God did choose King James, it was an odd choice and reflects adversely on the Almighty's executive ability.

James was the son of Mary, Queen of Scots, which isn't the

best start in life a boy could have. We aren't nearly so certain as to who was his father. Presumably he had been sired by Mary's husband, Lord Darnley, but the gossips claimed his father was in fact an Italian named David Rizzio, the Queen's secretary, although all they had to go on was that Darnley himself had helped murder Rizzio in the Queen's presence four months before James was born and had intended to murder the Queen, too, but for some reason didn't, which he probably wished he had because a little later on she murdered him. The Scots didn't mind this too much as they didn't care particularly for Darnley, but when Mary began catting around with the Earl of Bothwell, they said adultery was unscriptural and packed her off into exile, and crowned James King.

James was just a little boy at the time and, without a father or mother, was raised by a bunch of men and a dotty old countess, so he turned out about as you would expect.

James liked hunting, theological arguments, and being King, but he liked being King best. We have no reason to suspect that his firm belief in a Supreme Being was less than sincere, because if there isn't any God there can't be any divine right of Kings, and the divine right of Kings is what James really believed in. In fact, he was batty on the subject. He thought of the divine right of Kings as the fundamental fact of the universe, and considered it his sacred duty to popularize, promote, establish, and batten down this doctrine. It got so that when he started spouting off about it people began to figure ways of getting out of the room, much as people duck out of a boring cocktail party today. Many reliable historians say that by his performance in office King James I did more than any other one King to undermine and help destroy the doctrine of the divine right of Kings.

James loved theological disputation because he had read

some theology and wanted to show off his knowledge. Also, he thought he was much better at theological argument than bishops, let alone mere clergymen. For all we know, he may have been better at it than they were.[1] James was also afflicted with pockmarks, gimpy legs, and halitosis.[2] In addition, he suffered from irregular sexual preferences. Although he was married to a dumb blonde named Anne and dutifully produced progeny and referred to his wife as "my dearest bedfellow," all the time, much to the embarrassment of the decorous types who hung around the Court, he really liked boys better. His last great love was a toothsome young fairy named George Villiers, and the way they carried on was almost too much of a scandal even for a King, and Kings can stand more scandal than ordinary people.[3]

Also, as an administrator James was awfully bad even as Kings go, which is pretty bad. He had a knack of always making the wrong decision at the wrong time, then acting on it in the most inept and bungling manner open to him. The only thing which saved the Empire from degenerating into a complete shambles was that James was monumentally lazy, preferring almost anything to work. Thus, he would habitually put off doing anything about one crisis after another because he had a ball to attend or a theological argument to indulge in, and by the time he got around to doing something about

[1] The Church of England has never been very strong on producing first-rate theologians. This is because the C. of E. clergy spend so much time riding to hounds or drinking tea with the duchess.

[2] In seventeenth-century England almost everybody had halitosis.

[3] James once blubbered that "Christ had his John, and I have my George." As a Stalwart Christian, this made James feel a lot better about the whole thing.

these pressing problems there wasn't anything he could do about them, so they turned out much better than if he had done something.

But we are being picky. What if James did have a minor defect or two? After all, none of us is perfect, and he was a staunch and Stalwart Christian, and no one can deny that he is responsible for the Authorized Version of the Scriptures, which is a Stalwart Christian contribution if there ever was one.

Not that James did the actual translating because he had too many balls to attend and too much hunting to do so he didn't have the time, though he didn't doubt that he could have done it if he had wanted to.

The King James Bible came about almost by accident. The Church of England was carrying on a rousing battle between the High Churchmen and the Puritans, and though James didn't particularly appreciate the High Churchmen as they thought the King should really be under the authority of the bishops and James knew that the Church should be under the authority of the King, he didn't appreciate the Puritans too much, either, as they reminded him of the knotheaded Presbyterian clergy back in Scotland. One of the reasons he had been glad to move to England as King was to be rid of the contentious Presbyterian clergy in Scotland.[4] On January 16, 1604, some High Churchmen and some Puritans were meeting with the King at Hampton Court[5] outside London, as the plague was laying everyone low in London at the time. The

[4] The other reason he had been glad to move was that in Scotland he was a poor King, whereas in England he was a rich King.

[5] Cardinal Wolsey had built Hampton Court, but Henry VIII had swiped it from him. It has a thousand rooms.

meeting was for the purpose of settling some of the ungodly quarreling in the Church of England.[6]

They didn't settle the quarreling, but somewhere in the discussion Dr. John Rainolds, president of Corpus Christi College, Oxford, and a Stalwart Puritan Christian, butted into the conversation and said, "May Your Majesty be pleased to direct that the Bible be now translated, such versions as are extant not answering to the original."

Since this had been proposed by a Puritan, His Grace the bishop of London felt obliged to take the other side of the suggestion and huffed that "If every man's humor might be followed there would be no end to translating," which, it is hard to deny, is a sound idea and might have carried the day as the King didn't like Rainolds very much.[7] But the King also fancied himself a Bible scholar, and couldn't resist adding his learned opinion which was, "I profess I could never yet see a Bible well translated in English, but I think that of Geneva is the worst."[8] He didn't think much better of the Coverdale, or Bugs Bible (so named because it translates Psalm 91:5 as "Thou shalt not nede to be afraid of any bugges by night") nor of the Bishops' Bible (popularly known as "the Treacle Bible" because it translates Jeremiah 8:22 as "Is there not treacle in Gilead?"). The King's low regard for the Geneva

[6] The Puritans and the High Churchmen were kicking up a dust over such fundamental issues as whether the communion table was a table or an altar, and whether people could have picnics and things like that on Sunday.

[7] Sir John Harrington was at this meeting, and wrote to his wife that "The King talked much Latin and disputed with Dr. Rainolds." Sir John has also gone down in history as the inventor of the privy.

[8] The Geneva Bible is also known as the Breeches Bible because it translated Genesis 3:7 as "and they sewed fig leaves together, and made themselves breeches."

Bible maybe was because he found its English clumsy and inaccurate, but more likely because some of the Geneva's marginal notes did not speak highly of the divine right of Kings, which was proof enough to James that it was an heretical translation.

Nothing more was said about the Bible project, as James had to hurry to Royston for the bustard shooting, which was reported to be excellent at that season, and then to London to watch a fight between three dogs and a lion. The lion won, tearing two of the dogs limb from limb. The other dog then declined to fight any more. But in the meantime Bishop Bancroft, who had opposed the Bible project because nothing good could come from a Puritan, saw which way the wind was blowing and took it upon himself to get the project under way. Besides, the Archbishop of Canterbury had just caught a bad cold and died, and Bishop Bancroft, desiring wider opportunities for serving the Lord, thought that being Archbishop of Canterbury was probably what the Lord had in mind for him. The trouble was that several other bishops thought it was what the Lord had in mind for *them,* so Bancroft needed a gimmick to promote his candidacy and concluded that the Bible project was just the thing. It was, too, because he beat out everybody for the job, including Lancelot Andrewes, Dean of Westminister, whom everybody thought ought to have it.

Fifty-four scholars were finally selected for the job, although others helped, and some of them had to be replaced as now and then they would die during the six years it took to do the job.[9] They were divided into three groups which

[9] Edward Lively, professor of Hebrew at Trinity College, Cambridge, who had thirteen children and was always broke and being

met at Westminister, Oxford, and Cambridge, and the chair-
men of these groups had a hell of a time getting them together, getting them to work, and getting them to agree.
Although Bishop Bancroft wrote to a friend that "You will
scarcely conceive how earnest His Majesty is to have this work
begun," James wasn't earnest to the point of planning to pay
the scholars anything as he needed all his spare cash for
masque balls and bustard shooting. He did graciously con-
sent to give all the vacant "livings" (rectorships of churches)
with a halfway decent salary attached to the needy scholars,
which was generous of him although it didn't cost him a
farthing since he had to give them to somebody anyway. Also,
several of the translators, including a few of the Puritans, were
able to promote themselves bishoprics as a reward for their
services.[10]

Among the more interesting of the translators, or "learned
men" as they are sometimes called, were:

The aforementioned Dean Lancelot Andrewes, the only
name among the learned men remembered much today.
Hardly anybody today knows he helped translate the Authorized Version, but he wrote some prayers which were collected
and became one of the most popular devotional books of all
time.[11] Dean Andrewes was known as a gentle, kindly man
who read and spoke fifteen languages, and who urged the

---

sued, was the first of the scholars to die. He kicked off in May of
1607 with "an ague and a squinsey."

[10] The Puritans were opposed, on principle, to bishops because
they said it was contrary to God's will that there should be bishops.
However, when they had a chance to be a bishop, they saw that
perhaps it wasn't contrary to God's will that there should be
bishops.

[11] Among Stalwart Christians, Catholic or Protestant, devotional
material has always sold a lot better than works of scholarship.

King to execute Bartholomew Legate for holding Unitarian views, which the King did, burning him on March 18, 1611, shortly before the King James Bible was published.

Dr. John Rainolds, who suggested the project in the first place. He was said to be the most learned man in England, who thought it was sinful for people to play "mum chance and maw," to dance around the maypole, or to indulge "with wenches" in stool ball, which was a sort of cricket played at Eastertime between men and women, with the winner getting a pudding flavored with tansy juice.

Laurence Chaderton, a Puritan, who enjoyed brawling in the streets at Cambridge, married the daughter of the Queen's wine merchant, and lived to be 103.

Dr. Hadrian Saravia, the oldest of the learned men, and said to be "a terrible high churchman." Dr. Saravia was King James' favorite translator because Saravia was very strong on the divine right of Kings.

The Reverend Richard "Dutch" Thompson, rector of Snailwell, Cambridgeshire, of whom one of his fellow translators said, "He is a debauched drunken English Dutchman who seldom went to bed one night sober," but who could evidently handle his booze because he never had a hangover.

Dr. Miles Smith, who served as editor and wrote the preface, wrote tracts on the desirability of the clergy being well paid, and ended up a bishop.

John Bois, who didn't like his wife much, was an amateur doctor who was forever reading books about diseases and then thinking he had the latest disease he read about. He also picked his teeth all the time.

George Abbot, a sour, pious old bastard who wrote a book called *A Brief Description of the Whole World,* and later killed a man.

Andrew Bing, who outlived all his fellow translators.

The Stalwart Christian translators bickered among themselves continually, and competed for churchly honors, and shirked their work, and, all in all, it is a wonder that the King James Bible ever got translated at all, let alone well. When it finally got printed in 1611, the first edition averaged about one typographical error every ten pages, among them translating Ruth 3:15 "and *he* went back into the city" when it should have read "and *she,* etc.," which caused the people to name it the "he Bible," and when the error was corrected in later editions, they named the corrected version the "she Bible."

Although it sold pretty well from the start, everybody complained about it, saying such things as they didn't think the language was elegant enough, that it didn't conform to the original texts, that it taught heretical and un-Christian doctrines, and that it was in every way greatly inferior to the older translations such as the Bugs Bible and the Treacle Bible.

There have been several translations of the Bible since the King James, of course, including the Revised Standard Version and the New English Translation, both of recent years. When they were published, modern Stalwart Christians said, and are still saying for that matter, that these new translations don't use elegant enough language, that they don't conform to the original texts, that they teach heretical and un-Christian doctrines, and that in every way they are inferior to the King James Bible.

Anyway, the late H. L. Mencken, a stalwart atheist, and an acknowledged judge of the use of language, declared the King James Bible a work of art. "It is," he said, "probably the most beautiful piece of writing in all the literature of the world."

So whatever else you may say about it, King James' Stalwart Christian committee did what no other committee before or since ever did—produced a work of art.

We don't know exactly what King James thought of the translation, but it is safe to say that he liked the front page because it had his name on it, and he probably found nothing offensive in the rest of it because the King James Version does nothing to undermine the doctrine of the divine right of Kings.

Sören Aabe Kierkegaard

We know that Sören Aabe Kierkegaard was a Stalwart Christian because he said that he was. He thought he was the only one left—in Denmark, at least. He was born at Copenhagen in 1813, and died there in 1855, which means that he had a relatively short life. Considering all his trials and tribulations, it probably seemed longer. Sören was known as S.K. in Copenhagen then, and in the better egghead circles today.[1] His father called him "the fork."[2]

[1] He was called S.K. in Copenhagen because those are his initials. He is called S.K. by contemporary eggheads because it is the in thing to do. A pseudo-intellectual will say "as Kierkegaard once wrote . . . ," but the genuine article always says, "I recall that S.K. said . . ."

[2] Some say because of Sören's smarty-alecky conversational manner his father said he had "a forked tongue," shortened to "fork"

Sören's father, M. P. Kierkegaard, was fifty-six years old when Sören was born, and had been retired for sixteen years, as he had made a packet in the dry-goods game. He was a very religious and very melancholy man. We don't know why he was religious, but he was melancholy because, as a poor shepherd boy on the heaths of Jutland, he had once cursed God,[3] and because after his first wife died, he started sleeping with the housekeeper. He had to marry her before the year of mourning was up as she was beginning to show. Her name was Anne Lund, described as "a cheerful little woman," and she didn't seem at all bothered by her informal arrangements with M. P. Kierkegaard, although he felt very melancholy all the time and said his life was lived under a curse because he had bedded her without benefit of the clergy. Also, he felt that Jehovah was pretty mad at him for cursing the Almighty, so M. P. Kierkegaard had a galloping case of the spiritual blahs. Theologians call this sort of thing "a sense of sin," and are very enthusiastic about it and think everyone ought to have it, as evangelical religion thrives only when this sense of sin is present in abundance. Although M.P.K. never did get rid of his hangup over "carnal connection" with or without sacred ceremony, he didn't slow down too much, and Anne Lund produced babies with a regularity that would have thrilled the Pope, number seven in this line of progeny being S.K.

In addition to sex, M. P. Kierkegaard was quite fond of dialectic argument,[4] and had many friends who dropped in just to debate with him. Little Sören was fascinated by these

---

for convenience. Others believe the nickname derived from early evidence that Sören would be an accomplished trencherman.

[3] Jutland is not a very attractive place.

[4] He did not feel guilty about his passion for argument.

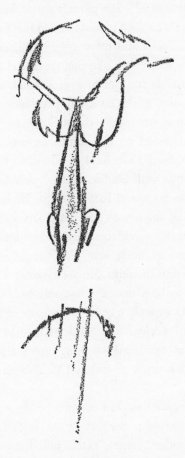

noisy sessions, which perhaps inspired him to develop his own abilities along these lines and eventually led him to a reputation as one of Copenhagen's wittiest conversationalists.[5]

In 1821 Sören entered the Borgersdydskole (which means

[5] Many saints (such as St. Anthony of the Desert) were canonized because they kept their mouths shut. Stalwart Christians, on the other hand, tend to be quite gabby.

"school of civic virtue"). His parents dressed him in sissy-style clothes, which no modern parents would think of doing as they have read Dr. Spock and other sound authors and educators and know how something like this scars a child's psyche and makes it impossible for him to ever amount to anything. But there weren't any works on child psychology back then, so S.K.'s psyche was scarred by the nickname "choirboy" which his classmates pinned on him. Since he was a little kid and rather delicate, he did not think it advisable to try to beat up on his tormentors with his fists as the other boys were pretty husky, although he would have liked to. So he confined himself to smacking them with his sharp wit and ready tongue, and his schoolmates would then beat up on him.

When he was a young man, S.K. would often sit around thinking ponderous thoughts. He once wrote:

"One ought to be a mystery, not only to others, but also to oneself. I study myself; when I am weary of this, then for a pastime, I light a cigar and think." Theologians and philosophers consider this kind of thing great fun. They would rather do it than drink or watch TV. This is why they seem strange.

M. P. Kierkegaard wanted his two younger sons to make a career of the Christian ministry in the state Church of Denmark. Sören's older brother, Peter, sailed through his education and eventually became a bishop. Sören did very well at the university until he passed his examination in the Arts and Sciences, which permitted him to choose his own courses and progress toward his examination in theology at whatever pace he chose. So he spent the next ten years going to lectures, but mostly engaging in extracurricular activities and being a gay blade. He writes that during these years he was always "dressed in the latest fashion, with a cigar in my mouth." He also carried a cane.

We are told that S.K. was a popular campus figure, especially among the literary and intellectual types. He gained a reputation as a brilliant conversationalist and a creator of witty sayings. He also drank a lot.

His brother, Peter, was disgusted with Sören, and commented that "Sören does not seem to be reading at all for his examinations." We might not be shocked by this, but Peter also said, "Sören is mixing with poets and the like."[6]

Outwardly S.K. appeared to be gay, happy, and carefree. He knew he was smarter than almost anybody, and he reveled in his social success. But this was only a façade. Inwardly, he was miserable, unhappy, and, like his father, given to extended bouts with melancholy.[7]

When he was twenty-two years old, S.K. found out about his father's premature liaison with Anne Lund, and immediately became an atheist. Freud would have been able to explain this, but it is best that we don't try to figure it out. Right away he decided that Christianity and philosophy cannot be reconciled.[8] Also, he wrote a long article exposing Christianity as a hoax. He did this, he said, to tell people what a terrible thing Christianity is and "to warn everybody whose breast is not enclosed in such spiritual corsets not to let themselves in

[6] Society has always considered mixing with poets an infallible symptom of an unstable character.

[7] A certain amount of inward misery is necessary if one is to become a Stalwart Christian.

[8] Even when he gave up atheism and became a Stalwart Christian, he remained unshakable in his distaste for philosophy. There is probably a reason for this, but research has not revealed it.

for it carelessly, in order to protect them against such narrow-chested, asthmatic notions."

Somewhere it is written that men's lives turn on one or two pivotal events and experiences. One of these events occurred to Sören Kierkegaard when he was just getting warmed up as an atheist. He visited a house of ill-repute and had sexual relations with a prostitute. He claimed that he was drunk at the time, and that anyway the other fellows talked him into it, but this is what boys always say. The experience convinced him that he had inherited his father's powerful eroticism, for which he thought he ought to feel terribly guilty. He never quite got over it.[9]

Not long after this small taste of sin, S.K. attended a high-brow literary reception. He was, conversationally, in top form. Sinning had not dampened his wit. Kierkegaard's favorite university professor, one Paul M. Moller, listened to his former pupil spout off for a while, and then said, "Sören, you are so through and through polemicalized that it is perfectly frightful."

To you and me this doesn't sound like much of a remark, but later S.K. referred to it as "the trumpet of my awakening," and saw it as the point when he turned from atheism back to Christianity.

Though determined now to become a Stalwart Christian, S.K. found that it wasn't all that easy. He had to give up his evil companions, he thought, so he gave up all companions. This didn't work out. He got lonesome. He did continue to steer clear of intellectuals and other undesirables, though. In his postatheist period he said that he liked best talking with

[9] Some people can handle such an experience, and some can't.

"old women who retail family gossip, after them with lunatics —least of all with very sensible people."

S.K. made remarkably rapid progress toward becoming a Stalwart Christian. Less than a year after Professor Moller's remark which was the agent of his conversion, S.K. wrote a sermon on the moral and spiritual decadence of western Europe,[10] a positive sign of his improving emotional and spiritual health.

Kierkegaard was still hostile to his father, and in September of 1837 decided he could no longer live under the same roof with the old sinner, so he found a pad of his own. He had the wit, though, not to be hostile to his father's money since he had no immediate plans for earning any of his own. He consented to accept around a hundred dollars a month from M. P. Kierkegaard for living expenses. He also permitted his father to pay off his accumulated debts for the past two years. These amounted to about six hundred dollars in liquor bills, a hundred or so for tobacco, a substantial charge account for "clothing and haberdashery," and a whopping nine hundred dollars for books.[11]

We have evidence that S.K. enjoyed, during this period of his life, steady spiritual growth because he went around saying things like "My life is, alas, all too conjunctive, would to God I had some indicative power" and "*Idées fixes* are like a cramp in the foot—the best cure is to stamp on it."[12]

[10] Stalwart Christians always point out that they are living in spiritually lousy times. This is one way you can tell a Stalwart Christian.

[11] It is comforting to know that while S.K. was a drunk, he was an exceedingly well-read drunk.

[12] When making statements Stalwart Christians like to sound profound. It is not important for us to understand what they mean.

Other significant events during S.K.'s early postatheist period included a reconciliation with his father, the passing of his theological examinations at the University, and falling in love.

The most important of these events was falling in love. The girl was named Regina Olsen. Her father was a government official, and she was fourteen years old when Sören fell for her.[13] Kierkegaard's courtship of Regina was a long, painful, embarrassing process, and it is best that we don't go into it too fully as it would only remind you of an Ingemar Bergmann movie.

There can be no doubt that Sören was mightly smitten with Regina. In his journal for February 2, 1839, he wrote: "[Regina] Thou sovereign of my heart treasured in the deepest fortress of my breast, in the fullness of my thought, thus when it is equally far to heaven and to hell—unknown divinity! Oh, can I really believe the poets' tales. . . ." There's plenty more, but this will give you an idea of how he felt. You have to be pretty far gone to write such stuff.

S.K. harbored no doubt that the fair Regina would tumble into his arms at his slightest beckoning. Excessive modesty about his own abilities was not one of S.K.'s vices. What did bug him was his own sinfulness and an uneasy feeling that it might not be God's will for him to marry Regina.

So he put off declaring his passion to its object. But he did moon around quite a lot. He found out where Regina took her music lesson, and on the appointed day stationed himself in "a second-class coffeehouse" across the street so as to catch glimpses of her coming and going. He spent so much time in

[13] Girls mature early in Denmark. What else can a girl do during those long, cold winters?

this coffeehouse, in fact, that his friends took notice and he had to think up a story. He tells us that he "represented to them that the coffee was the best in the whole town. I even exhorted them with much pathos to try it."[14]

Things went from bad to worse. S.K. began dropping in at the Olsen home, usually bringing Regina some nuts and books. The nuts were gifts, but he made it plain that the books were strictly on loan.

S.K. finally got around to proposing and, as he expected, Regina said "Yes." But the next day he was convinced he had made a mistake to contract for a marriage, not an uncommon reaction in newly betrothed males. After a decent interval, he broke the engagement and went off to Berlin to hear a series of lectures by the philosopher Schelling and to feel melancholy. But he kept Regina's letters in a rosewood pedestal, which is much better than keeping a girl on a pedestal, although we are afraid that S.K. did that, too. He also dedicated a book to her. It was titled *Two Discourses at the Communion on Fridays,* which must have given her a big thrill.

S.K. spent the rest of his life writing books and inventing Existentialism. (He wrote standing up at a sort of tall school desk, although we don't know why. The desk has been preserved and can be seen in the Kierkegaard room of the City Museum of Copenhagen if one cares to see it.) In his writing he was unrelenting in his attacks on the state Church of Denmark, but the Church didn't seem to mind.

He also wrote things like ". . . when I see a fly settle down in a crucial moment on the nose of a businessman, or see him bespattered by a carriage . . . or a drawbridge opens before him, or a tile from the roof falls down and strikes him dead,

[14] A few of them did try it, and thought S.K. had flipped.

then I laugh heartily. And who could help laughing?" and "I would rather gamble, carouse, fornicate, steal . . . than take part in making a fool of God."[15] This sort of writing may strike us as unexceptional, but it was considered to be provocative stuff in nineteenth-century Copenhagen. Although people frequently got pretty worked up over the stuff he would write and call him dirty names and things like that, he really didn't change anybody's mind or start any new schools of thought in his own day. It took nearly a hundred years for people to get excited about S.K.'s stuff, which is why it is said that S.K. was sadly neglected in the nineteenth century but has become the most influential philosopher of the twentieth century. And though it would be difficult to back this up since several hundreds of philosophers think they are the most influential philosophers of the twentieth century, it is safe to say that S.K. is very big as a philosopher today.

On October 2, 1855, he went to the bank and drew out his remaining capital, and on the way home suffered a stroke on the street. When they got him to the hospital, he said, "I have come here to die," which he did.

John Wesley

If it weren't for John Wesley there would be no Methodist Church today, which some people think would be just as well. He was born June 17, 1703, the fifteenth child of Samuel and

[15] So would most people.

Susanna Wesley,[1] and his full name was John Benjamin Wesley,[2] but he didn't like the Benjamin part of it and never used it, so practically nobody has ever known what his middle name was.

Wesley's father was rector of the Church at St. Andrew at Epworth, a rather crummy little town in Lincolnshire built on what had once been marshland before the Dutch or somebody drained it to improve it, but it didn't improve it much. Samuel Wesley was rector at Epworth for thirty-nine years, but his congregation didn't care a great deal for him. They said they didn't like him because he was a Tory, and he said they didn't like him because they were a bunch of stupid, ignorant lunkheads who couldn't appreciate a scholarly sermon. At this late date it is impossible for us to tell who was right. Sometimes the people would express their disapproval by burning the rector's crops, and once they burned his house down. John was about five years old when the house burned, and he was sleeping on the third floor. They got everybody else out except John, and when they saw him at the window Samuel Wesley couldn't think of anything to do but pray, which he did, kneeling in the courtyard in his nightshirt—not a particularly edifying sight. But some men, who saw that the rector was taking care of the praying, climbed on each other's shoulders somewhat after the fashion of an acrobatic troupe on The Ed Sullivan Show and got little John out just as the roof fell in. For the rest of his life John took this as a sign that he had been saved by God for a special purpose in life, and re-

[1] They finally quit at nineteen.

[2] He was named after his brother John and his brother Benjamin, both of whom had died before he was born. This seems to us an odd way to name a child, but we have to remember that by the time you have had fifteen children you tend to run out of names.

ferred to himself as "a brand plucked from the burning," although he had quite a bit of trouble discovering exactly what God had in mind for him.

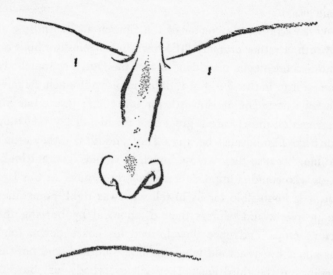

From all the evidence we have, John was very fond of both his father and mother, so he can't be explained in terms of Oedipal complexes or mother fixations or other hangups of which modern psychologists are so fond. His mother had more influence on him, though, because his father spent all day in his study writing a terribly learned commentary on the Book of Job, which is unfortunately out of print, but which was on the press as the old man lay dying, and which, as a good Tory, he dedicated to Queen Caroline, who was a rather dizzy dame to begin with and she also drank a lot.[3] Susanna Wesley had a low opinion of the schools of the day so she educated her

[3] When John presented a copy of the book to her, the Queen said, "My, what a pretty cover," and laid it aside. Not everyone, of course, is fascinated by commentaries on the Book of Job.

children at home, and contrary to what you would expect, they all turned out pretty well.

John went to Charterhouse School in London as a "poor scholar," meaning that somebody else had to pay the freight, and though nobody noticed him then, the school has bragged ever since that he went there and has tried to cabbage on to a little of the credit for making him into what he became.[4] He got along fine at Charterhouse, and a few years later it is recorded that he was honored by being named as one of the stewards for the school's founders' day dinner. As a steward he was supposed to plan the menu and engage the cook and waiters and musicians. The menu he selected was as follows: roasted pike, fried whitings, flounders, spitched eels, shrimps, tongues, udders, pigeons, venison pasties, chines and turkeys, lamb and ragouts, wild fowls, sweetbreads and asparagus, almond tarts, roasted lobsters, pear tarts, sirloin of roasted beef, fruits, jellies, custards, and florentines, and plenty of various wines to wash it all down.[5] Wesley was not a big eater,[6] but the custom of the day was gourmandizing on a

[4] The poor scholars were known as "gown boys" because they had to wear broadcloth gowns lined with baize, which made it easy to tell them from the "town boys," who paid tuition and didn't wear gowns.

[5] Stalwart Methodists today—American Methodists, anyway—are violently anti-booze and point out that Wesley was, too, which he was, being very hostile to the use of gin and spirits except in cases of extreme necessity. But he did not consider wine and beer as booze. Wesley advised his preachers to take a small beer before retiring, which is one part of the Wesleyan tradition not emphasized in American Methodism.

[6] He claimed he once lived for four years on nothing but potatoes. This sounds somewhat monotonous to us, but perhaps he liked potatoes.

grand scale. Horace Walpole described a lady of the time who was supposed to be the epitome of feminine pulchritude much as Elizabeth Taylor is admired today, or was before she began running to fat, as having "two acres of cheek spread with crimson, an ocean of neck that overflowed and was not distinguishable from the lower part of her body." Thackeray said that "Swift was fat, Addison was fat, Gay and Thompson were preposterously fat; all the fuddling and lunch drinking, that club and coffeehouse boozing, shortened the lives and enlarged the waistcoats of the men of that age." King George III was a tub of lard.[7] Spitched eels and udders do not strike us as absolutely necessary to a well-rounded diet, but they ate some pretty strange things in eighteenth-century England.

Wesley went from Charterhouse to Christ Church College, Oxford, but though he still felt like a brand plucked from the burning, he didn't know why. In 1725 he decided to be a Church of England clergyman like his father, a decision which pleased his mother but which his father didn't think was such a hot idea.[8] But he gave in and even wrote John a lot of advice as fathers are wont to do. He told John to devote himself to prayer and study, and also told him not to waste time with Bible commentaries as none of them were any good.[9] John was soon ordained, but was apparently in no screaming hurry to become a parish pastor and pulled all the political strings he could to land a job as college professor, and was taken on as a fellow of Lincoln College, Oxford. He soon received his master's degree, and to celebrate the occasion, he delivered three lectures the same day entitled "De Anima Brutorum,"

[7] His favorite meal was cold mutton and salad, plovers' eggs, stewed peas, and cherry tarts.

[8] He had hoped that John would amount to something.

[9] His Bible commentary wasn't published yet.

"*De Julio Cesare,*" and "*De Amore Dei,*" which must have been most exciting. Honors poured in upon him. He was nominated to preach the sermon at St. Michael's Church on St. Michael's Day, became lecturer in Greek and philosophy, and was appointed claviger, which means keeper of the keys of the treasury, of Lincoln College.

John Wesley had always considered himself a good Christian. Unlike some saints and Stalwart Christians he had never gone in for helling around, so when he became a clergyman and decided to become also what he called "a real Christian," he had nothing in particular to repent of, which he found something of a handicap. Like practically all Stalwart Christians, though, he concluded that his main business was to save his own soul from everlasting damnation. Since he couldn't repent to good advantage, he had to figure out some other way to make the grade, so he practiced being pious and limited his friends to those whose spirit and conversations were "likely to lead me on the way to heaven." He was especially grateful to one friend, he told his mother, who had shown him how foolish are the pleasures of life, and thus presumably gave him a healthy boost along the difficult road to heaven.

As a part of his soul-saving strategy Wesley thought he ought to suffer some, so he took a parish church. Actually, he agreed to serve as his father's curate and be pastor to a little church attached to his father's living at Epworth. This place was out in the bogs, accessible only by boat, and was called Wroote-out-of-England. John's sister Hetty described the people at Wroote in a little poem:

> High births and virtue equally they scorn,
> As asses dull, on dunghills born,
> Impervious as the stones their heads are found,
> Their rage and hatred steadfast as the ground.

One would gather that this was not a particularly intellectual congregation. John Wesley stood them for four years, but concluded that there must be other ways of saving his soul and left. He never had anything to do with the parish ministry again, and after Wroote-out-of-England he never could work up any enthusiasm for the country or country people.

So John Wesley went back to Oxford, which was not noted as a godly place, but it was better than Wroote-out-of-England. He did discover that there were some godly goings-on, though, at Christ Church under the direction of his younger brother Charles, who had come up as a student while John had been trying to save his own soul out in the bogs of Lincolnshire. Charles was the leader of a group of students who met regularly for prayer and Bible study and other pious activities. John immediately joined the group, took over the leadership as he did with any group he joined, and put godliness on a highly organized, systematic basis. The unregenerate students thought this was a riot and called the group variously the Reforming Club, the Godly Club, the Holy Club, the Sacramentarians, the Bible Moths, the Supererogation Men, and the Enthusiasts, all original and creative names, demonstrating the advantages of an Oxford education. Unlettered and ignorant people never would have thought of them. One extraordinarily brilliant student whose name, regrettably, has been lost in the mists of history, said one day, no doubt peering through his monocle at the group trooping to its prayers, "Jove, I do believe we have here a new sect of Methodists sprung up," or something like that, and the name stuck. Wesley and his holy chums also spent several hours each week visiting the prisons and preaching to the prisoners which, unlike most good works, seems to have been greatly appreciated by those worked on.

One would think that all this methodical piety and good works would have filled John with spiritual pride and moral superiority as it does with most people, but unfortunately he was still worried to death over the salvation of his soul. So, with his brother Charles in tow, he went out to General Oglethorpe's colony in Savannah, Georgia, in hopes of converting the Indians. This project proved to be a disaster as John got involved with a girl named Sophia Hopkey, whom he thought he wanted to marry, then decided he didn't, and when she expressed her irritation by marrying someone else, John wouldn't let her come to communion, or maybe he wouldn't let her come to communion and then she married someone else—it's all very confused. Anyway, he never did convert an Indian,[10] so he went back to England.

Back at Oxford, with his soul still in a state of sad disrepair, Wesley was convinced that since he didn't have any faith, he had better give up preaching, a not illogical conclusion. He consulted Peter Böhler, a Stalwart Christian of the Moravian sect, and Böhler said Wesley was making a mountain out of a molehill. The thing to do, Böhler said, was to "Preach faith till you have it, and then, because you have it, you will preach faith," which seems to us a kind of reverse brainwashing self-taught, but it worked just dandy. Wesley began preaching here and there and people came by the thousands to hear him, and before he knew it he had a mammoth religious revival going with himself as the head of it.

You and I wouldn't have cared to live in eighteenth-century England, as all serious-minded people of the time saw it as the worst society in the history of mankind. The poor people were

---

[10] He did try, but the Indians said that as they were engaged in some wars at the moment they wouldn't be able to find time to listen to the gospel.

awfully poor, and drank all the time. The rich people were awfully rich and drank all the time.[11] Everybody was greedy, and business ethics were not all they should have been, and thieves and murderers and worse more or less did as they pleased because there were so many of them you couldn't catch and hang anywhere near enough to make much difference.

There were plenty of churches and preachers around, but this was the Church of England founded by that Stalwart Christian King Henry VIII, and you know what it was like. Just in case you don't, perhaps we should explain that back then the priesthood of the Church of England was a happy haven for the estateless younger sons of the nobility who weren't qualified to earn a living by working, and didn't want to anyway as this would have disgraced the family name. And back then bishops weren't selected for their piety, learning, spirituality, good judgment, and qualities of leadership as they are today, because then if you wanted to be a bishop, as nearly all clergymen did inasmuch as there was usually a fine salary attached to the job and the work wasn't strenuous and people had to address you as "My Lord Bishop," what you had to do was play politics, and nobody cared if you were qualified or not.

Lord Sandwich once had a dozen Church of England clergymen as dinner guests and bet them that every one of them had a corkscrew in his pocket but that there wasn't a prayer book among them, and won. The bishop of Winchester

[11] The poor people drank cheap gin, on which they could get drunk for a penny, and dead drunk for two pennies, a bargain much envied by dedicated drunks today. The rich people got drunk on fine French wines, as cost was not an important consideration to them.

was known to have held examinations for candidates for ordination while watching a cricket match. The same good bishop was supposedly more skilled and more frequent in his use of profanity than any British seaman. When reprimanded for his excessive swearing, he would reply that he swore as a baronet and not as a bishop. The King's mistress sold a bishopric for five thousand pounds. A first-class bishopric paid in the neighborhood of five hundred times as much as the average salary of a clergyman in one of its parishes, and parish priests often doubled as the keeper of the local pub in order to make ends meet.

From all these facts, it would seem unreasonable to have expected the Church of England to save eighteenth-century England, and it didn't. John Wesley did.

A modern Stalwart Christian anxious to save society would go in for berating the social system, picketing Parliament, plumping for reform measures and new laws to aid the poor, and in extreme cases proposing things like the guaranteed annual wage, free medical care, and similar hairbrained socialistic schemes.

Not Wesley. What he and his revival did was to make people feel better about being miserable. Wesley learned that nothing made miserable people feel better than a superheated sense of sin. He described in his journal a mass meeting at Bristol in which "the terror and confusion were inexpressible . . . the people rushed upon each other with the utmost violence, the benches were broken in pieces, and nine-tenths of the congregation appeared to be struck with the same panic." At another meeting he says of the congregation, "Some of them, perhaps many, scream all together as loud as they possibly can. Some of them use improper, yea, indecent expressions in prayer. Several drop down as dead, and are still as a corpse. . . ." As anyone can see, this was all great fun and a good time was had by all at the Wesleyan meetings. It is hard to understand why Wesley himself was never ecstatic over these manifestations of religious enthusiasm, and we must regretfully conclude that he never quite got over his snobbish preference for dignified prayer-book religion. But though he may have found the whooping and hollering which accompanied his preaching distasteful and the thousands and tens of thousands who came to hear him,[12] always indulging in religious high-jinx and getting saved and in general racing around and falling all over each other something of a bore, Wesley could comfort himself that his converts went off the sauce,[13] and found their daily existence, while no less miserable, much more tolerable. Members of the Methodist sect were sought as employees by the mill and colliery owners because they soon noticed that Methodists showed up for work sober, had a low rate of absenteeism, and murmured not at all about the starvation wages and long hours.[14]

Wesley's foothold in anything resembling an organization, since the Church of England of which he was a priest would have nothing to do with him and wouldn't even let him preach in their churches, was among the Moravian Christians and their society at Fetter Lane, London. But he fell out with them because, he said, they weren't really as stalwart in their Christianity as he had at first thought, and also one of the

[12] You probably think this is stretching the truth because there wouldn't be any churches big enough to hold all these people. There weren't. Wesley did much of his preaching outdoors, in fields, at the entrances to mines—places like that.

[13] With such delightful substitutes as faintings and paroxysms and holy groanings, who needs it?

[14] Employers notice virtues like these quicker than anybody.

leaders of the Moravians named John Bray was preaching that no one could be a true Christian unless he was a Moravian Christian, which Wesley wasn't.[15] The Moravians said Wesley fell out with them because he wanted to run everything himself, and they wouldn't let him.

At any rate, Wesley decided that a Stalwart Christian awakening such as he was carrying on needed a headquarters, and he bought an old foundry off City Road, London. He got it cheap, only 115 pounds, because a few years before a workman named Schalch had told the boss it was going to blow up and the boss said nonsense, British foundries didn't blow up, but it did, killing the boss and a goodly number of the workmen and doing the building no good. Wesley remodeled it into a chapel seating fifteen hundred,[16] and also rooms for prayer meetings and an apartment for himself, and lesser accommodations for the other preachers in his movement who popped in now and then for a breather before they hit the road again.

Church historians like to stress that Wesley's real genius is shown in his tremendous organizational idea embodied in the Methodist societies. Like all great ideas, it is very simple in concept. You take eleven Methodists and one Methodist leader and you have them meet once a week, and you have a number equal to the twelve disciples, and there is no telling what spiritual wonders will come out of it. This is essentially the cell idea, which all good Communists and anarchists are so

[15] To Wesley's credit, he never claimed that the only true Christian was a Church of England Christian, but he did think the C. of E. was vastly superior to the other brands of Christianity then on the market.

[16] Men and women had to sit in separate sections so as not to distract them from hearing the gospel.

devoted to and which they probably copped from Wesley. It is beyond question that the concept of the Methodist society is what got Wesleyanism off the ground, because you can have all the big meetings you like with everyone getting sozzled on religious ecstasy, but when the meeting is over what have you got? You have to organize and manipulate people if you expect to have a first-class religious awakening, or any other movement for that matter. Wesley saw this clearly, and has gotten credit for it in history, but it wasn't his idea. A Captain Foy, otherwise undistinguished in the annals of mankind, proposed the society idea strictly as a money-raising gimmick at a time when the Wesleyan awakening was strapped for cash.

"I'll tell you what I'll do," he said. "Just give me eleven Methodists to call on every week and I'll collect a penny from each of them, and maybe some others will do the same, and we'll soon be rolling in dough."

It was soon discovered that there would be less wear and tear on the leaders if the members of the societies would just get together once a week and bring their money with them, and this has been the basic financing idea for all non-tax-supported churches ever since.

What Wesley liked best about the society concept, though, was that if you had leaders of every eleven Methodists, and then you had a sort of superleader over a batch of the leaders, why then it was quite easy to tell everybody what to do if you were the leader of the superleaders. Wesley thought and thought as to who would be the best qualified leader to be the leader of the superleaders, and the only person who fit the job description was Wesley himself. Wesley soon turned these leaders into lay preachers with quasiministerial status, and even for his superleaders he had many lay preachers, although he did get an occasional Church of England clergyman to join up. With this kind of organization it wasn't long until all England was well salted if not downright saturated with the Methodist religious awakening.

Wesley had two overriding passions: his desire to see that a person's soul was saved, and after that was taken care of, to improve their earthly existence along the lines of his own convictions as to how other people should live. His ideas as to how other people should live were remarkably similar to how he lived. To condense his philosophy of life, he believed that everyone should be sober, industrious, obedient to authority, a good Tory as to political loyalties, clean,[17] pious, temperate in food and drink, decent but somber in dress,[18] and many other things which you can easily guess. He was also a bug on education. He thought everyone ought to be educated so they could appreciate the classics and his sermons. He started schools and Sunday schools so the poor would learn to read. And he believed that books, which in those days were invariably big and expensive, ought to be small and cheap, so he launched a publishing venture and invented "the reader's digest" by cutting what he considered fluff out of the classics and other big books he had published, an idea which some people say is a boon to mankind and others don't.

Some historians insist that the Methodist revival wouldn't have gotten to first base had it not been for Charles Wesley, John's younger brother. Charles was supposed to have been a preacher with lungpower superior to John's, but it was as a poet that he made his real contribution to the Methodist awakening. You may think a poet is the last thing a religious awakening needs, but you would be wrong. You simply can-

[17] He coined the phrase "cleanliness is next to godliness," which has done so much for soap sales ever since.

[18] Methodist ladies were not supposed to wear jewelry.

not prod people out of their spiritual snoozing without zippy hymns for them to sing, and if all you have in the way of hymns are metrical versions of the psalms and similar soporific stuff, you have to write some of your own and then steal some popular tunes of the day which have real spiritual potential when joined with good religious words. This is what Charles Wesley did. As a matter of fact, he ground out around sixty-five hundred hymns, which is an average of a hymn a day for twenty years with very little time off for Sundays or holidays, so what if he did tend to repeat himself?[19]

His work was somewhat uneven. No one but an oaf can rightly criticize

> All praise to our redeeming Lord,
> Who joins us by his grace,
> And bids us, each to each restored,
> Together seek his face.

On the other hand, not everyone is inspired by such lyrical sentiments as

> Ah, lovely appearance of death!
> No sight upon earth is so fair.
> Not all the gay pageants that breathe
> Can with a dead body compare.[20]

[19] Charles Wesley wrote two hymns which begin "And am I born to die?," three which begin "Author of faith," and thirty which start out with the word "come": "Come, holy spirit," "Come, humble sinner," "Come, Holy Ghost" (there are three "Come, Holy Ghosts" plus four "Come, Father, Son, and Holy Ghosts"). We must remember, though, that it isn't easy to think up sixty-five hundred different ways to start a hymn.

[20] One is surprised that the National Association of Undertakers has failed to adopt this as their official hymn.

But then, tastes differ. Is Wordsworth a lesser poet because once, in a weak moment, he wrote a line about duty being the stern daughter of the voice of God? Ought we remember Browning as the author of "Pippa Passes" instead of "My Last Duchess"? The trouble with being a poet is that the muse isn't always around when you need her, but you have to keep up your production anyway.

Charles, who was something of a snob and rigid in his High Church views, was also capable of writing nasty verse. He had one of his frequent fallings-out with brother John when John took it upon himself to ordain Dr. Thomas Coke a bishop before the doctor left to supervise Methodist work in the American colonies, which had just broken their connection with England.

Here we must pause to explain how bishops are made. All true bishops can trace their spiritual ancestry back to St. Peter, who, as everyone knows, was the first Bishop of Rome and therefore the first Pope. St. Peter, we know, ordained other bishops by laying his hands on their heads and saying, "You're a bishop," or words to that effect. Then these bishops did the same thing to other bishops, and so on, and so on, down to the present. This being a bishop going back to St. Peter is known as "the Apostolic Succession," and if you say you are a bishop but aren't in the succession, you just aren't the real goods. John Wesley, though ordained a priest by a bishop in the Apostolic Succession, wasn't ever ordained a bishop, so he couldn't ordain anybody a bishop, or at least if he did, which he did, it didn't count. John thought it was important to have a Methodist bishop in America even if you had to fudge a little in the matter of the Apostolic Succession. Charles thought nothing was as important as sticking by the

rules of the Church of England. So when John ordained Dr.
Coke, Charles wrote a little poem:

> How easy now are bishops made
> At man or woman's whim!
> Wesley his hands on Coke hath laid,
> But who laid hands on him?

People who weren't sympathetic to the Wesleyan revival,
which had been humping along for more than forty years
when this was written and consequently had had plenty of
time to make a lot of enemies as well as friends, greatly enjoyed this poem and the falling-out of the Wesley brothers.
But both John and Charles were old men by now, and old
men can be pretty crotchety and quarrelsome. However, they
soon patched it up.

There are scads of books on the life of John Wesley written
to inspire devout Methodists today, but most of them leave
out anything about his love life, or if they mention it, they go
over it very lightly. In view of the facts, this is just as well.

He got off to a bad start in the love department. His first
love was a Betty Kirkham, daughter of a clergyman in Glouces-
tershire, and he was so hot for her that her brother Robert,
a friend of John's at Oxford, talked as if John were already
his brother-in-law. But nothing came of it, and Betty married
a Mr. Wilson, who left no footprints on the sands of time.

Next came Mrs. Pendarves, who had married a fat and
gouty Cornish gentleman forty-three years her senior who conveniently drank himself to death by the time she was twenty-
three years old. Mrs. Pendarves was reputed to be quite a
dish, popular at Court, and had even been chased for a while
by Lord Baltimore who, cad that he was, didn't marry her.

John had it bad for Mrs. Pendarves and wrote her some silly letters,[21] but she ended up marrying a Mr. Delaney.

Then there was Sophia Hopkey, of whom we have already spoken, and heaven knows how many others there may have been whose names somehow leaked out of history before John found his true soulmate, a young widow named Grace Murray. John actually proposed to her which, so far as we know, he had never done before. He told her God intended her to be his wife, perhaps not the most romantic proposal on record, but she was all aflutter over it and replied, "This is too great a blessing for me, this is all I could have wished for under heaven." Once she had him bagged, she didn't want him out of her sight, so she became his traveling companion through Yorkshire and Derbyshire and Ireland, a period of several months, and Wesley said she was "unspeakably useful" to him during this time although he didn't explain exactly what he meant. After they returned from Ireland, they were "scarce separated" in five months of traveling around the country. It occurs to us that a pious evangelist traveling with a comely widow in tow is slightly irregular, but evidently it caused no scandal at the time, and even Wesley's bitterest critics didn't seem to think there was anything out of the way going on between the two, which may be a compliment to Wesley or may be an insult, depending on your point of view.

The trouble started when Wesley announced that he was going to marry Grace Murray. His brother Charles had recently married a woman of the upper classes, and he was horrified that John planned to marry a woman who had once

[21] In their correspondence John called her "Aspasia," which wasn't her name, and she called him "Cyrus," which wasn't his name. If this makes you a little queasy, try to remember that passion tends to unhinge the mind.

been a servant. He raised cain with John and claimed that it would be the end of the Wesleyan religious awakening if its leader married "so mean a woman."[22] John said he was going to marry her anyway, but he didn't because she up and married another Methodist preacher named Bennet, which upset John no end, so he took to writing poetry about unrequited love, a sample of which reads:

> Oft, as through giddy youth I roved,
> And danced along the flowery way,
> By chance or thoughtless passion moved,
> An easy, unresisting prey,
> I fell, while love's envenomed dart
> Thrilled through my nerves, and tore my heart.

There are thirty more stanzas to this, and they get worse and worse.

Wesley finally got married when he was forty-seven or forty-eight years old—at least old enough to have known better—to a widow with four children named Mrs. Vazeille, who was "a woman of sorrowful spirit," according to one of her acquaintances. One would have thought that experience would have taught him something and that by this time he would have been a little leary of widows, but it hadn't and he wasn't.

We don't know much about the courtship except that Wesley fell while crossing London Bridge and sprained his ankle so bad he couldn't walk, and for some reason went to Mrs. Vazeille's place in Threadneedle Street to recuperate, and before anybody knew what happened and before he could walk on the sprained ankle, he was a married man.

And if you think this wasn't such a thrilling courtship, wait

[22] Some of Charles' best friends were servant girls, but he didn't want his brother to marry one.

until you hear about the marriage. Mrs. Wesley combined a violent temper, a raging jealousy, and a malicious spirit, any one of which is bad news in a wife, and put together with throttle open, which is how she operated most of the time, are enough to drive a man to drink in no time. Since Wesley didn't drink very much, or care to, he traveled a lot. She would swipe Wesley's papers and give them to his enemies, or add words here and there to change the meaning of what he had written and make it sound bad and then publish it in the papers. She went through all his mail and raised the devil if she found a letter, no matter how innocent, from some female. She once imprisoned John and Charles in a room and went on and on giving them hell for their faults, and they might have been there yet except that Charles started quoting Latin poetry at her, and no one can stand listening to Latin poetry for very long at a time, so she let them out.

We have preserved one of Wesley's letters to his wife in which he lists ten things he wishes she would do differently. Among them are to quit making him a prisoner in his own house, stealing his money, talking about him behind his back, lying, swearing, and so on. One of Wesley's preachers, John Hampson by name, said he once went to see the Wesleys and found Mrs. Wesley foaming with rage and pulling Wesley around on the floor by his hair. Hampson said she even had a fistful of hair in her hand which she had pulled out of his scalp, which seems an unlikely story unless we remember that Wesley was a little guy, hardly topping five feet, and so light a brisk zephyr would blow him away, so a husky old bag such as Mrs. Wesley must have been would have no trouble at all bashing him around.

Mrs. Wesley was always picking up and leaving John, vowing never to return. But John, who for some reason never did know when he was well off, always begged her to return, which she would do and take up where she had left off, only meaner. After thirty soul-corroding years which Wesley once described as

> Like drops of eating water in the marble,
> At length have worn my sinking spirits down,

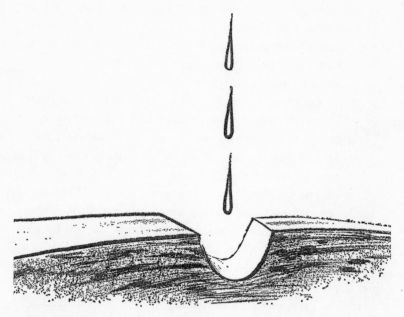

she had the grace to expire without any particular trouble to her husband, as he was off on a trip at the time. His only comment was, "I came to London and was informed that my wife had died on Monday. This evening she was buried, though I was not informed of it till a day or two after," so he didn't have to go to her funeral and weep or in other ways make a hypocrite of himself. She is buried in Camberwell Churchyard, where her epitaph reads: "A woman of exemplary piety, a tender parent, and a sincere friend"; but says nothing whatever about her being a good wife. Wesley did appreciate her, though, because he told his friend Henry Moore that probably God had made Mrs. Wesley bitchy in order that he would want to stay away from home all the time and carry on the great work of the religious awakening instead of hanging around the house and enjoying life like his brother Charles did after he got married to his high-born but evidently agreeable wife.

His titanic achievements as a religious leader have somewhat obscured Wesley's tremendous contributions to the sciences. He published a book on psychiatry, and a book on electricity, and even invented a machine to give you electric shocks for the good of your health, a sort of puny forerunner of today's electric shock therapy which does the same thing, only gives you a much bigger jolt.

But it was in the field of internal medicine that Wesley really shone. He published a work called *Advices with Respect to Health Extracted from a Work of Dr. Tissot* in which he said a doctor who bleeds his patients, which all doctors did back then, is nuts.

But his *Magnum Opus de Medica* is a book called *Primitive Physic or an Easy Method of Curing Most Diseases*, a bestselling title if there ever was one, and indeed it was one because the first edition was brought out in 1747 and the last in 1839. The author has in hand a copy of *Primitive Physic* which was brought to America in 1832, and whose tattered pages make for reading more fascinating and fully as edifying as that current repository of avante garde medical knowledge, *The Reader's Digest*.

Wesley tells us in the preface that there was no need of

medicine before the fall of man, as Adam and Eve dwelt in a disease-free world. But as punishment for sin and to fulfill the Scripture "Dust thou art, and unto dust thou shalt return," God in His goodness has seen fit to afflict us with all manner of ills, most of which can be mitigated by following Wesley's advice.

The natural source of disease, he says, is creation, that "the heavens, the earth, and all things contained therin, conspire to punish the rebels against their Creator." Therefore, he says, the sun and moon shed unwholesome influences from above, and the earth exhales poisonous damps from beneath, and the beasts and birds and fishes are in a state of hostility toward man. Furthermore, the air we breathe is "replete with the shafts of death," which, of course, no resident of New York City or Chicago or Los Angeles will deny for a minute.

One would think that, in the light of these chilling facts, Wesley would have appreciated the medical profession, but he tells us he has a low opinion of doctors except, of course, the God-fearing ones, which apparently weren't too numerous back then. Doctors like to act as if they are gods and are privy to knowledge so esoteric that only they can grasp it, Wesley says, so that they can keep a monopoly on the practice of medicine and increase their incomes. He also thinks the drug business is a racket, and that the doctors conspire with the apothecary to prescribe twenty medicines where one will do. Thus, he felt compelled to write his book.

He lists diseases in alphabetical order, with numbered paragraphs under each heading containing possible cures. The idea is to try paragraph one, and if that doesn't work, try number two, and so on. He begins with Abortion (to prevent) and ends with "Of Purges and Vomits," which comes just before his "Table of Medicines."

You might need to know sometime what you should do if you come down with a quartan ague, which would be to apply to your wrists a plaster of turpentine, or if turpentine isn't handy, a plaster of bruised pepper and treacle. Or when afflicted with St. Anthony's fire, a glass of tar-water every hour will do wonders. Baldness may be cured by rubbing the deforested pate with onions, which might make you smell funny but is reputed to be most effective.

Under "C" we come to "Consumption," for which Wesley specifies ten cures. The tenth on the list reads "In the last stage, [make love to][23] a healthy woman daily. This cured my father."[24]

It is impossible for one man to spend over fifty years saving so many people in so many different ways and not collect a host of critics, backbiters, jealous friends, and downright enemies.

The historian W. E. H. Lecky said of the Methodist religious awakening that "a more appalling system of religious terrorism, one more fitted to unhinge a tottering intellect and to darken and embitter a sensitive nature, has seldom existed."

Leigh Hunt, the poet, wrote an essay titled "On the Indecencies and Profane Rapture of Methodism," which is not exactly complimentary to the Wesleyan awakening, as you might guess from the title. Hunt was offended by the esthetic quality of Methodist depiction of the Deity in sermon and song,

[23] Wesley does not use the euphemism "make love to" which we think it is better to use here. He used a simple, four-letter Anglo-Saxon word which today you hardly ever find in medical books but which occurs frequently in the graffiti on the walls of comfort stations.

[24] Later on Wesley himself almost died of consumption, but miraculously recovered from it and was as good as new.

and thought he detected sexual symbolism and other disgusting things in it. "The Deity is personified and embodied in the grossest of images," he complained. "If God must be addressed in the language of earthly affection, why not address him as a parent rather than a lover?"

Admirers of the Methodist movement point to the stabilizing influence the movement had on British society and claim that by making the English working class sober, industrious, submissive to the established order, and content with their miserable lot here because their hope was to have a high old time in the sky bye and bye, Methodism prevented a revolution in England. Critics of the Methodist movement say exactly the same thing.

Though there have been plenty of critics of Methodism in England, there aren't any in America because it is in America that Methodism bloomed into its fairest flowering. It is generally conceded that the Methodist Church is the church which best typifies the true American spirit. It is rich and fat and highly organized and slightly puritanical and conservative in politics and anti-intellectual and rigidly authoritarian in structure, blessed with numerous bishops and numberless board secretaries to give orders and devise programs and tell the people what to think and what to do so they won't be troubled thinking for themselves, and thousands of submissive and obedient parish pastors grateful to do the bidding of the bishop and their congregations at wages a plumber's apprentice would scorn.

Though John Wesley conceived his religious awakening as a movement for the benefit of the lower classes, Methodism in America doesn't have to fool around much with the lower classes any more because it has been smart enough to become the religion of stalwart middle-class Christians[25] and move to the suburbs—and wouldn't John Wesley, were he alive today, be proud of Methodism's success?

[25] The middle-middle class, that is. The lower-middle class is still Baptist and Lutheran, and the upper-middle class is an impregnable fortress of Presbyterianism and Congregationalism.

The Stalwart Christian Syndrome

The dictionary tells us that a syndrome is "a group of symptoms that together are characteristic of a specific condition, disease, or the like," which leads us inevitably to the conclusion that a syndrome is what Stalwart Christians have, and if we can only break it down into its components, we might profit immeasurably from discovery and imitation.

The author has not forgotten that it is the secular lessons, not the religious, we wish to learn from our Stalwart Christians because it is the secular benefits, not the pious, which we seek. Happily for us, these secular lessons are no less abundant in the lives of the Stalwart Christians than they are in the lives of the saints.

Let us keep in mind that the Stalwart Christians we have studied, along with hundreds of others we could have inspected to our profit except for the limitations of space, achieved, whether they aimed for them or not, such highly prized secular goals as leadership, wide public acclaim, power enough to boss everybody around, the privilege of hobnobbing with other celebrities of the time, and at least a nodding acquaintance with Kings and lesser royalty. And to a man they bagged for themselves a permanent place in history. About all they didn't do that we might think they ought to have done was to make pots of money for themselves, a grievous oversight from our point of view. However, in defense of our Stalwart Christians we must recall that each and every one of them could have made pots of money for himself if he had wanted to. John Wesley, for example, did in fact rake in the dough from his writing and publishing in amounts sufficient to win respect from a Wall Street banker. That he gave it all away instead of spending it or putting it in the stock market, while odd, shouldn't be held against him. The significant fact is that the Stalwart Christian Syndrome enabled him to make it by the barrel, and the ability to make it by the barrel has always been one of the most exalted of secular virtues. How a man spends it after he has made it is considered, even in the least pious of circles, to be his own business. Do we think less of Andrew Carnegie because he frittered away millions on libraries? Is anyone contemptuous of the Mellons or the Fricks because they collected art? We all admire the avarice of a Daniel Drew, but does he merit our scorn because he endowed a Methodist seminary?

Let us look, then, for the qualities which, added together, not only made our Stalwart Christians Stalwart Christians but made them what is more important: unquestionable and resounding successes. These guys were winners.

Scrutiny reveals some marked differences between the methods of pleasing the Almighty employed by the saints and those favored by Stalwart Christians. By and large, the saints were passive in their approach, content to be mystics, contemplatives, virgins, and the like. In other words, they thought the road to paradise is best traveled by sitting still.

The Stalwart Christians, on the other hand, went loping along to glory by doing something. They wanted to change things, and were forever reforming this or that, and liked to push people around. They meddled in politics and fiddled with thought control and often fancied themselves as economists and sociologists as well as theologians.

From this we deduce that an important cog or grommet in

the Stalwart Christian Syndrome is a vast liking for telling other people what to do. The casual reader will conclude, for example, that John Calvin was being capricious and petty when he passed an edict against the wearing of slashed breeches in Geneva. Indeed, it seems to us that the wearing of slashed breeches threatened neither the morals nor the security of the city. But that is beside the point. What counts is that John Calvin thought it did, considered his judgment superior to the collective judgment of the Genevese, and made it stick.

Not many of us want to be the dictator of a theocracy, or to write fifty-nine quarto volumes of theology which Calvin was and did. But many of us do want to be head man at the advertising agency, or president of General Motors, or chairman of the House Ways and Means Committee. Any of these or similar aspirations demand, as a prerequisite, a taste for telling everybody what they must buy or drive or do.

These Stalwart Christians also were not in the least diffident about letting the world in on what they thought. While the saints, with some notable exceptions, thought highly of silence as an aid to their assault on heaven, the Stalwart Christians talked all the time. To say that they were loquacious is equivalent to remarking that Denny McLain pitches well or that Twiggy is on the slender side. It vastly understates the case. When you contemplate the number of sermons and lectures Wesley and Calvin delivered, for example, it boggles the mind. Sören Kierkegaard had no pulpit or public platform, but he was so entranced by the sound of his own voice and the quality of his wit and wisdom that he was a nonstop conversationalist and could run off at the mouth for hours on end.

And when they did shut up for any length of time, these Stalwart Christians would go off to their studies or somewhere and write something. They were, in fact, compulsive writers. It was as if they believed that sheer volume and weight of printed material would serve to impose their ideas on mankind, and it would seem that they were right. The basic principle here is that people will think you are right if you tell them often enough that you are right. Calvin's Doctrine of Predestination, for example, has only a limited appeal when it is reduced to a paragraph or two, but after reading fifty-nine volumes, or even, say, only thirty-five volumes on the subject, you are likely to see more in it than you had initially believed possible. To demonstrate the applicability of this principle to secular endeavors, we need only look at the modern advertising industry, which has a thorough grasp of it, and which has perhaps carried it to ultimate efficiency in the television commercial. To persuade anyone that there are substantial differences among competing brands of soap flakes or cigarettes would appear, on the face of it, an utter impossibility because, in fact, there are no substantial differences among them. But by telling us often enough that there are differences where we know there aren't, we are brought to a state in which we would rather fight than switch.

Someone is bound to point out that Thomas de Torquemada was a Stalwart Christian leader who neither said much nor wrote anything (except, perhaps, orders for torture and execution). But we must not forget that his was a special situation. It was not at all necessary for him to convince the general public that his ideas should be listened to and acted upon. All he had to do was convince the King and Queen, which was, apparently, ridiculously easy.

So if you combine a relish for telling other people what to do with endless repetition of your ideas, you can expect, no matter what the enterprise to which you set your hand, at least modest and maybe even spectacular success.

But for a brass-bound, copper-riveted guarantee of secular success, you have to take that extra step which the Stalwart Christian leaders took, add that unique ingredient which they always added. It is, in fact, the identifying mark, the essential gimmick, the indispensable part of the Stalwart Christian Syndrome, and it is this: Always—let us repeat, always—identify what you want or the way you think things ought to be with the unchanging will of the Almighty.

We recognize that this isn't easy to manage. A person may like to tell people what to do, and be ever so loquacious, but then some latent timorous quality will assert itself and prevent him from taking this final, decisive step which ensures beyond any possibility of slipup that victory will be his.

John Wesley never really got to first base as a Stalwart Christian until he got over wondering what was God's will for his life and decided what it was. He couldn't even convert one lousy Indian in Georgia because he wasn't sure what he was doing there in the first place. But after he was sure that what John Wesley wanted was at all points identical to what Jehovah desired, he was able to persuade people by the tens of thousands to give up drinking and other pleasant ways of spending time in exchange for long, hard work at starvation wages and listening to two-hour sermons—a task we would have thought entirely beyond the bounds of possibility. Luther's early years were spent in a spiritual sweat agonizing over his acceptability to God and confessing all the time. But once he saw, though, that he was not only acceptable to God, but had in fact been chosen by the Almighty to speak with the authority of heaven, he was able to start wars and snarl up the Holy Roman Empire and set princes and Kings and Popes at each others' throats, and accomplish other beneficial things. And we can be certain that Torquemada and Calvin would have been unable to burn people at the stake or lop off their heads had they not possessed an abiding conviction that they were burning and lopping in the name of Christ.

The author realizes that the countless thousands who read this book must come to the end of it filled with gratitude that the incalculable benefits to be derived from a study of the lives of the saints and other Stalwart Christians have been called to your attention. A mastery of this text enables you to discard all other how-to-succeed books, for it is a complete library in this field. A thorough reading of it makes it unnecessary, indeed superfluous, for you to enroll in a Dale Carnegie course, or even spend the time and money to graduate from the Harvard School of Business.

Since gratitude must needs be expressed, the author will appreciate your letters of praise, along with anecdotes about how the saints and Stalwart Christians rescued *you* from the mud of mediocrity in which you had been wallowing and set your feet on the firm path toward secular success.

A better way, though, to express the thankfulness now welling up in you would be to pass along the good word. Be an evangelist for the cause. Don't lend this book, for it should never be out of your possession. Buy ten copies, or, better yet, a hundred, and give them away to relatives, friends, pastors—anyone needing to be rescued as you have been. Think of the good you can do!

True enough, such a program—if adopted by enough grateful readers—will result in substantial accruals to the author's royalty account. But let no one accuse the author of selfish motivations, for he intends to devote these profits to a number of worthy causes which he has in mind but feels it is better not to specify at this time. And anyway, it was no less a Stalwart Christian than St. Paul who said, "Who serves as a soldier at his own expense? Who plants a vineyard without eating any of the fruit? Who tends a flock without getting some of the milk? . . . the plowman should plow in hope, and the thresher thresh in the hope of a share in the crop."